SPEECH

AND

SOCIETY

SPEECH
AND
SOCIETY

THE CHRISTIAN LINGUISTIC
SOCIAL PHILOSOPHY OF
EUGEN ROSENSTOCK-HUESSY

———————————

George Allen Morgan

with Comprehensive Bibliography
by Lise van der Molen

UNIVERSITY PRESSES OF FLORIDA
University of Florida Press / Gainesville

Printed in the USA on acid-free paper. ∞

Library of Congress Cataloging in Publication Data

Morgan, George Allen, 1905–
    Speech and society : the Christian linguistic social
philosophy of Eugen Rosenstock-Huessy / George Allen
Morgan : with comprehensive bibliography by Lise van der
Molen.
        p. cm.
    Bibliography: p.
    Includes index.
    ISBN 0-8130-0852-2 (alk. paper)
    1. Rosenstock-Huessy, Eugen, 1888–1973.   I. Title.
BX4827.R57M67   1987
191—dc19   87-16038
                                                                  CIP

UNIVERSITY PRESSES OF FLORIDA is the central agency for scholarly publishing in the
State of Florida's university system, producing books selected for publication by
the faculty editorial committees of Florida's nine public universities: Florida
A&M University (Tallahassee), Florida Atlantic University (Boca Raton), Florida
International University (Miami), Florida State University (Tallahassee), Univer-
sity of Central Florida (Orlando), University of Florida (Gainesville), University
of North Florida (Jacksonville), University of South Florida (Tampa), University
of West Florida (Pensacola).
    ORDERS for books published by all member presses of University Presses of
Florida should be addressed to University Presses of Florida, 15 NW 15th Street,
Gainesville, FL 32603.

TO

MARGARET R. T. MORGAN

Ella guardava in suso, ed io in lei.

CONTENTS

PART THREE: FIRES OF INSPIRATION

PROLOGUE

EUGEN ROSENSTOCK-HUESSY (1888–1973) is one of the deep-est and most original thinkers of our time. He is also one of the most difficult.

I came to know him in 1934, when I was in the midst of writing *What Nietzsche Means*. I found his conversation fascinating, or-dered his books from Germany, and read them eagerly. He struck me as a man of genius, full of striking insights, his lan-guage wonderfully alive.

At the same time his language was more puzzling than that of anyone I had read, far more than Nietzsche's. Flashes of meaning would catch my eye, then disappear around the corner before I could focus on them. It was clear that he was not getting through to his readers as he should.

So in 1939 I offered to help him prepare a book that might be more readily understood. He agreed, and the result of our colla-boration was *The Christian Future*, the most widely published of his writings.

Long before it appeared I left philosophy to become an infantry private in World War II, then spent the next quarter-century in the Foreign Service. So I had little time to read his later writings until I retired. In 1970 I began reading them and soon decided to try to understand his thought thoroughly, hoping to write a book and share my understanding with others. Since 1972 this task has absorbed all my time. The present volume is the result.

Born in Berlin, the son of a Jewish banker, Rosenstock-Huessy became a Christian in his youth. Obtaining a doctorate in law at Heidelberg, he began a brilliant academic career, becoming the youngest *Privatdozent* in Germany as a member of the Faculty of Law at Leipzig. His field was medieval constitutional law. But World War I, during which he served in the German army, interrupted that career with a profound shock that sent him far beyond his field in a search for the fundamentals of human history and destiny that lasted the rest of his life. During the war that search found expression in his famous correspondence with Franz Rosenzweig.

When the war ended and Germany was swept by revolution, he underwent an acute spiritual crisis, which led him to decline attractive religious, academic, and governmental offers. Instead, he devoted himself to founding and editing the first factory magazine in Germany, at the Daimler-Benz automobile plant. Then he founded and headed the Academy of Labor in Frankfurt, a venture in adult education. In later years he was elected vice-chairman of the World Association for Adult Education. In 1923, however, for financial reasons, he had to resume academic work, as professor of law at Breslau.

His activities and publications ranged far beyond law. He published a book on war and revolution in 1920, the first volume of his sociology in 1925, a three-volume work on the Church (with Josef Wittig, a Catholic) in 1927, and his most famous work, on European revolutions, in 1931. From 1926 to 1932, he organized voluntary work service camps, which brought together industrial laborers, farmers, and university students.

When Hitler came to power in 1933, Rosenstock-Huessy, who had foreseen someone like Hitler and who opposed everything Hitler stood for, left Germany, lectured at Harvard for three years, and then became professor of social philosophy at Dartmouth until he retired in 1957. Some of his most important works were published after retirement, and he lectured widely in Germany as well as in America.

Rosenstock-Huessy's early academic writings are fairly coherent, but when his vaster inspirations began bursting forth, he erupted like a volcano. He told me he had suffered agonies from having too much to say. He often started a train of thought, then digressed to another, and may or may not have pursued the former in another paragraph, another chapter, or another book. He made unqualified statements that he qualified elsewhere. I think he was unaware of the difficulties he caused his readers because the whole of his thought was vividly present to his own mind like a map. During our collaboration on *The Christian Future*, when I raised questions he was never at a loss for a prompt answer.

I believe, therefore, that he had in his mind a fairly coherent body of thought that never attained corresponding coherence in print. He described himself as having a system but writing in a post-systematic manner, always alert for new insights. He wrote as the spirit moved him at the moment and hence was not always consistent.

Like every original thinker Rosenstock-Huessy developed a language of his own. My greatest teacher, Alfred North Whitehead, was much criticized for his innovations in terminology, but he rightly held that to use familiar terms only would be to get caught in conventional ruts of thought. I have taken immense pains to learn Rosenstock-Huessy's language by studying instances of usage. Even so, I am unable to understand a large part of what he wrote, partly because the contexts fail to clarify the meaning of terms adequately. The present volume offers what I could pull together out of this fertile chaos. I hope it will help others to discover more of the insights still buried there. I tried to write chapters about many important topics, e.g. the ages of man, spirit, values, truth, and law, but was unable to bring the material to a focus.

The main themes that pervade Rosenstock-Huessy's thought are language, society, time, history, and Christianity. Instead of sociolinguistics, which studies language in its social context, he developed a linguistic social philosophy, which found clues to society in language.

In the pages that follow, I write as if Rosenstock-Huessy were speaking to the reader, reserving my comments for the epilogue and the notes, which often indicate problems still unresolved. All substantive statements in parts 1 and 2 are supported by passages cited in the notes. Many statements in the text are direct quotations. Some sequences may seem less than convincing, and many statements will raise further questions in the reader's mind, as they do in mine. The text goes only as far toward coherence and clarity as the evidence seems to warrant.

I have developed a vast index (with accompanying notes) of Rosenstock-Huessy's works; it is too long to publish, but it will be made available to scholars at a suitable library.

For many kinds of help in preparing the present volume, I wish to thank Professor Harold M. Stahmer, Professor Harold J. Berman, the Dutch scholar Lise van der Molen, Dr. Hans R. Huessy, Rosenstock-Huessy's son, and Margaret R. T. Morgan, my wife.

O N E

FUNDAMENTALS

CHAPTER 1

SPEECH THINKING:
THE GRAMMATICAL METHOD,
THE CROSS OF REALITY

LANGUAGE IS NOT merely a means to express thoughts, a mere tool: "all genuine speech remakes both listener and speaker—a fact that propagandists ignore, thinking they can catch men without themselves being caught." Speech "is wiser than the thinker, who believes he is thinking where he is only 'speaking' and thereby trusting the authority of the linguistic material." "... all future discoveries ... formulated by the 'speech thinkers' are hidden in this heresy against the Enlightenment, the mental rationalists .... It says that speech makes and breaks us, that we are contained by it, confined by it, redeemed through it." Speech is "the field of energy within which man receives or loses his mind, changes or opens it."[1]

As "the circulation of articulated speech is the lifeblood of society," and "grammar is the self-consciousness of language," the clue to human society is the grammatical method. In the future it should become the basis of sociology. Not all social relations involve language, of course, but the more enduring ones do. Language interacts pervasively with all other social institutions.

3

The whole of living language is the sole authentic system of human relations.[2]

The grammatical method, however, cannot be based on traditional school grammar. A new grammar is required if it is to be the organon of the social sciences in the third millennium of the Christian era, as mathematics became that of the natural sciences in the second. It must be "higher grammar," like higher mathematics.[3]

Traditional "lower grammar" is "the most obsolete and poisonous element in our social instruction." It rattles off tables of conjugation and declension as if all forms were on the same level. Higher grammar is hierarchical; it recognizes that there are important social differences, e.g. between saying "I love" or "you love" or "he loves." Lower grammar is Ptolemaic, centered around the individual speaker at one time and place. Higher grammar brings a Copernican revolution by emphasizing the social character of speech, including listeners as well as speakers and reaching into all times and places. It begins with imperatives, not indicatives. It is "empirical grammar" in that it makes "you" rather than "I" the first person because it is experienced first in a child's life; a child is addressed long before it learns to speak. This is "the most important reversal of the current superstition" about language: "through the fact that half the time I am listening . . . my mind vibrates as part of the twin body, and all my members and senses are given me anew . . . . They had led out from me, now they lead into me."[4]

For higher grammar, the proper sequence of persons of the verb is "you," "I," "we," "it," as normal experience moves through these phases. To these correspond four moods: imperative, optative or subjunctive, narrative, and indicative. The moods may also be called dramatic, lyrical, epical, and logical, as well as plastic, elated, conventional, and aggressive. Rotating continually through such phases, not skipping or getting stuck in any, constitutes "grammatical health" for societies as well as souls. Hence, the grammatical method also points the way to the diagnosis of and therapy for social illnesses. Modern factory language, for example, lacks the epical speech through which hatred is overcome by common narrative.[5]

"You" and the imperative are akin to the vocative by which persons are addressed. Lower grammar lists the vocative as the last case in tables of declension, but in actual experience it is the "pre-case" used ahead of the others. In fact, it is more like an imperative than a case, inviting the person addressed to turn toward the speaker and listen. In general, declension of nouns locates things in space, while conjugation of verbs orients events in time.[6]

Only names can be vocatives, obviously, and names are therefore the most important of grammatical forms. Not only lower grammar but modern thought generally makes the grievous mistake of failing to distinguish between names and ordinary words. In fact, the natural sciences amputate names, in this sense, altogether. The difference between names and words lies in how they function. The same linguistic element may be used as a name or as a mere word. "Words that have power are names." When a word is no longer used to move people or things, it has ceased to be a name.[7]

"A name is the point of intersection of three speech acts. First: I address you with it. Second: I talk about you with your name. Third (but now comes the most important approach to the crossroads that a name represents): I myself know myself by this name and in this name. I want to be able to have the same idea of myself as that which other people link with my name, and vice versa. Thus in a name three modes of existence of the same living, hoping, speaking and thinking (self-knowing) being cross each other. Nothing crosses in a a word. It merely labels an object." "A name generates a time-stealing tension between at least three speakers . . . . The name's field of force is itself a carrier of our life, a force that either keeps us alive or kills us. Since these names are high explosives, the new grammar is no playing with words." "The field of force of all historic struggles consists of the tension between the name that you give me and that by which I may demand to be addressed."[8]

Names are thus "the social life of language." Through them language is powerful, whereas mere words are powerless. Names are vehicles of spirit: they reveal social functions; they separate people and unite them. Names may have a limited span of life, but they are not arbitrary labels. While they live they are sacred because "they constitute the unity or the conflict of words and deeds." "The name is the right address of a person under which he or she will respond." "Words classify, but names orient . . .

personify ... incorporate ... into one society of communication. Without names communication would be impossible. For before two individuals may talk to each other in words about things, they must be mutually responsive, they must recognize each other as persons."[9]

Names as well as the persons and moods of the verb lead to the Cross of Reality, the comprehensive clue to social reality in which the grammatical method culminates. It represents a fourfold method of realizing (*vergegenwärtigen*) or encountering (*begegnen*) reality. With fewer than four approaches, we fail to grasp the whole of reality. Natural sciences, for example, describe only one fourth of it. They deal only with "objects" in complete detachment. The Cross is composed of time and space axes—future and past (preject, traject), inner and outer (subject, object)—thus pointing in four directions or "fronts," forward and backward, inward and outward. Take names, for example: some given in babyhood demand future deeds from the bearer. Family names characterize our historical origins. Some names belong to us as friends inside a community. Others identify us in relation to a hostile world in which we struggle for existence. Likewise, "you" and "we," "I" and "it," along with imperative and narrative, subjective and indicative, correspond to the axes of the Cross of Reality. "Through speech human society sustains its time and space axes." Being a method, the Cross is not static: "we ever draw anew the lines between the inside and the outside, tradition and progress."[10]

The Cross of Reality pulls us in four directions; hence, we are cleft and torn. "The Cross of Reality is an indelible pattern of conflict engrained in the very structure of all life . . . ." Hence, human life has to be social. "Only together can we man the various fronts of life adequately, stand the strain of decision that they entail, and bear the risk of the inevitable wrong choices which occur." " . . . being torn is a human privilege, because no society could develop among people who were self-contained."[11]

The sociological application of the grammatical method as Cross of Reality holds that "any living group, family, army, football club, nation, church cannot help spitting up in these four directions and delegating specialists for dealing with the new, the old, the external, and the inner life of the group." Four social evils represent failures on the "fronts" of the Cross: revolution, decadence, anarchy, and war. In revolution, the new generation uses violence against the old, the existing order. In decadence, the older generation lacks the faith "to inspire the next generation with aims that would carry them beyond themselves." In anarchy, as in an economic depression, people lack common inspiration and fail to cooperate. In war, states external to each other do not speak but try to exert power over each other. All four are diseases of language and hence of society—failures in communication.[12]

In addition to the Cross of Reality, the grammatical method leads to a vertical approach suggested by "hierarchical grammar," mentioned above. With regard to the Living Word, "he who hears is no longer his own subject: another authority reaches into him .... And he who commands is no longer concerned with mere objects .... The two new concepts contradict the horizontal approach of the schoolroom .... Hearer and commander can be understood only vertically as central values in a hierarchy of grammar." Such a hierarchy is illustrated by the three levels of names, words, and concepts, by the five levels of the spectrum of times (chapter 7), and by the three levels of God, man, and world of things (chapter 4).[13]

For the true sociologist (alas, not most sociologists today), human society is not known as the natural sciences know "objects" in the world of things. He realizes that he himself is a human being like those he studies and that he is a member of society, not a mere detached outside observer. He does not seek a system of *his thoughts about* people: "if a man made the whole of language come alive he would create the sole trustworthy system." The true sociologist relies on language for his work and people can talk back to him as well as with each other. Moreover, they are not fully knowable or predictable; he may say that they are going to do one thing, and they can decide to do something else. Also, sociology can and should influence its subject matter, unlike the natural sciences; it is a formative (*gestaltende*) science; it cannot be impartial, neutral, "objective." Its methods are based on the whole Cross of Reality. Thus, the sociologist "must step between backwards and forwards and thereby make up his mind as to what for him is past and done with, what is still a future necessity."[14]

The speech thinker finds in language the clue to life itself. Language is heightened life, the highest embodiment of life. It reveals the basic traits of all life in that it struggles against death, can turn against its own gravity and transform its own gestalt. "Speech conquers all the disintegrations and fissions that abound in nature and of which death is the most drastic form." "The complete unity of all men of all times, from Adam to the last Judgment Day, would be the greatest expression of our plenitude of speech." We overcome death by speaking beyond it: "language survives the bodily corpses of the mortals who speak." Love is stronger than death because we can love beyond death and love leads us to speak beyond it. "Only love, which impels us to speak, never faileth."[15]

CHAPTER 2

GODS, DEVILS,
THE LIVING GOD,
AND HIS GRACE

SPEECH THINKING LEADS to belief in God. We believe in Him when we speak, whether we realize it or not; even our doubts and denials presuppose His oneness. "The power to speak is God because it unites me with all men and makes us the judges of the whole world." Since God is omnipresent, He cannot be a mere object outside us. Asking if He exists is like asking someone, "Do you exist?"[1]

Gods are powers in our hearts that make demands on us and compel us to respond. They are inexorable. They make us speechless. The Bible calls them *elohim* in Hebrew. It is fashionable to call them values today. There are many, and they come and go in the lives of individuals and groups; science is no god for a child, and Venus abdicates her authority over old age. No god can enslave all the elements of our being or dominate any human life from birth to death. But there is One Living God of our future and our beginning who is "superior to the gods He has put around us in the short periods of our conscious efforts." Unlike them, He can be resisted. He lets us speak and He lets Himself be moved by entreaties. He invites us to obey "the one thing necessary and timely at any moment," thus liberating us from the compulsive gods. He calls us gently, and only compels us if we fail to hearken. He is the source of unity, including language, which unifies human life and the world.[2]

God "becomes known in our lives as the power of conquering death." The climax came with the crucifixion and resurrection of Christ: "death became the gateway to the future, to new life." "Jesus completed the revelation of the Living God because He created true future." "The Living God thus revealed by Jesus must be forever distinguished from the merely conceptual God of philosophers. Most atheists deny God because they look for Him in the wrong way. He is not an object but a person, and He has not a concept but a name. To approach Him as an object of theoretical discussion is to defeat the quest from the start. Nothing but the world of space is given in this manner." Philosophers start with space and try to be timeless, but God is known through an event that happens to us "only in the midst of living, after death in some form—bereavement, nervous breakdown, loss of hopes—has come upon us."[3]

"God does not emerge in the sphere of our reason; rather He is only the answer extorted by devils from a human being. If the devil becomes a comic figure," as in eighteenth-century deism, "God becomes a foolish, insipid decedent. Even the singular of the devil is a silly imitation of monotheism. There are many fallen angels." "For the last 150 years devils, the many gods, are claimed to be mere superstition." "Devils are simply gods that make their servants abjure God, who is above them." As God is the source of unity, the essence of deviltry is divisiveness, of which lying, the separation of thoughts, words, and deeds, is an example. "The devil is the 'primal no' that rips open the abyss of disconnectedness."[4]

That God is called the Living God does not mean that the gods are wholly dead. God overcomes death, disaster, and thus is the supreme degree of aliveness. The gods represent lower degrees. God is the creative process; He goes on creating; He did not merely create the world a long time ago. The gods are parts of His creation and in that sense derive from the past. God's creativity is the in-break of novelty from the future. He is inexhaustibly original. Gods repeat themselves, but God never does; His every act is done once for all.[5]

Gods can die, however. They live, to their degree, while they inspire a human group and are invoked by its members. When they cease to stand in the vocative and are treated as mere concepts, as the Greek gods were by the Alexandrian scholars, they are dead. God, on the other hand, dies for us because He would not be alive without dying, but He always comes to life again with new creativity. That is how He is eternal: not *immer* (always) but *immer wieder* (always again).[6]

Later chapters will show that gods were known to empires and Greeks, God to Israel and Christianity. But in the space-minded, world-oriented second millennium A.D., the rise of modern science and technology has led to pervasive industrialization and has made people "gods-less," rootless in the vast indifference of dead world-space. It is time for a rebirth of gods. They marry people with particular parts of the world—the forester and his forest, the poet with his language—which then become homelands, consecrated spaces of human hearts, instead of the dead space of physics. God's unity is so secure that a subordinate place can now be made for polytheism, gods as God's deputies to bring life and warmth again into an industrialized world.[7]

Gods are processes, not concepts, and hence encounter us in many forms. God also appears to the faithful in manifold ways: angry, silent, speaking, listening, and many more. It is dangerous to take His name in vain. "The Holy Trinity represents the maximum of simplification that Christianity has wrested from the panic of every believer in God." "The three Persons of the Trinity ... mark three paths through which God's full power is reflected." They are not separate individuals. "They are the three faces on which God continues to shine." We experience God when He overwhelms us in any of three ways, "as our Maker, as our Victim, and as our Vivifier."[8]

All humans pray, to gods or God, whether they know it and admit it or not. In times of crisis, when helpless and perplexed, they call on gods or God by name, and names, being reciprocal, give people orientation. The oldest prayers seem to have consisted simply of names. Israel staked its existence on establishing true prayer to the true God by distinguishing our will from God's will, thereby preventing relapse into magic and witchcraft. Prayer makes sense because God is free to create novelty, not bound by past or present. He can say "no" to our past and present selves. Through prayer we can learn who we are meant to be. Genuine prayer is an encounter of a human soul with its creator, in which it undergoes further creation. "Human prayers anticipate the inevitable, and by anticipating they create a field of force for liberty. Liberty is nothing but the taking of death into our lives. By anticipating death, we are delivered from evil."[9]

God's grace is a manifestation of His freedom, His free gift. It cannot be earned, bought, commanded, or organized by humans and it is not subject to any law. Humans are free in turn to misuse it and if they feel sure that they cannot fall from grace, they are already beginning to do so. Law means being recurrent, predictable, but grace is as surprising and unpredictable as the love that conveys it—God's love to man and the human love that answers by acknowledging it.[10]

Grace is God's creativity offered to human life. It brings the wholeness of a new quality of life, which can make possible and pervade a new period of living, another chapter in the creation of humankind. This wholeness consists of a unity of inspiration in which faith, hope, and love act together in the fullness, the entire spectrum of times, focused at first on a single human creature, now or never, here or nowhere. Life needs repeatedly to be made whole because of sin and death; old orders fall apart and decay. Grace brings redemption by teaching us to die to an old order at the right time.[11]

Grace moves in another dimension than law, stemming from heaven—God's future creativity—perpendicularly, as it were, down to earth (the lawful order already created). There it must have a second beginning among the existing human realities, where the gift must be accepted and where it gives rise to new laws through which it is carried out, forms a new order reshaping the old and valid for all. Otherwise, it blows away and is lost. In this context, the theological notion of grace as God's mercy for some who have broken His law is reversed; grace precedes law. Beginning uniquely, it becomes general. It comes once—for all. The series of its epochal formations, bringing whole new orders into human actuality, is the story of salvation. Medieval monks were carriers of grace into a worldly church and a clannish world torn by blood feuds. They were able to prepare a new social order because they left, were converted from, the old one.[12]

The process through which an act of God's grace is embodied in human living is called *revelation*. It begins with someone's private experience, but the experience has then to enter the world, to be made public. Worldly mentality, left to itself, would murder the new experience by judging it in terms of accepted concepts. The world is compelled to admit the new experience, alive and unfalsified, only by the sacrifice of a human life—as in Jesus' death on the cross—or by loving acknowledgment on the part of another person—as in Elizabeth's life-saving greeting, which meant that Mary's experience of the Annunciation was no longer private to her alone.[13]

CHAPTER 3

THE MULTIFORMITY
AND UNITY OF MAN

DIFFERENCES OF NUMBER yield further applications of the grammatical method to sociology. Our traditional grammar mentions only singular and plural, but Greek had a dual number and all languages generally also have collective expressions that are readily a fourth kind of number, though not marked by inflectional forms.[1]

To begin with the plural, the habit of talking about "society and the individual" suggests that society is a mere sum of atomic individuals. But in modern industrial society, despite its tendency to destroy traditional human groups, we find that factories have several men working as "molecules"—teams or other small groups—not separately as individuals, although that is how they are still regarded by management. Here we have people in the plural. The life of such molecules should be further developed and recognized by law. Their optimum size and duration should be determined. They should be given responsibility for performance as groups, develop self-government, and take pride in competing with other groups. This would give labor a dignity now lacking and would provide a sounder basis for the representation of the labor force than letting workers vote as individuals.[2]

Nations, political movements, sciences, and churches are examples of collectives. They tend to have far longer time spans than do or should factory "molecules." The latter deliver work wanted here and now. The former reach endlessly into past or future, offer escape from the limitations of present reality, and seek growth. They have elative, idealizing qualities and point toward common goals. "The collective deals with parts in relation to a whole, with positive facts in relation to a superlative." The collective use of a noun is such a superlative, e.g. "Youth" or "Labor." When such an idealized noun loses its intensifying collective quality, the idea dies. Young people have strong collectivist proclivities which could find a natural outlet in idealistic common service, illustrated by the work camps discussed in chapter 16. Communism carries this natural tendency to an extreme.[3]

The dual involves a relationship between just two; three or more would be plural, an entirely different quality. In the dual, dialectical opposites are brought together as polarities of a higher unity, as in true marriages of men and women. Instead of seeking their own interests, as in contractual relationships, the partners are devoted to each other and help each other to become more themselves. Such relationships lead to perpetuation, propagation, and regeneration. A proper marriage requires a period of courtship in which the differences are overcome and a common faith established. Unlike the shorter durations of the "molecule" and the far longer time span of most collectives, the dual of marriage normally lasts for the self-conscious half of a human lifetime, for a generation at least.[4]

With so much of life spent in the dual, plural, or collective, what is left for the singular? It is found in the soul, the biographic unity pervading all the phases of a human life from birth to death. "To outlast and to run through all these phases, aggregate states, combinations—childhood, work, play, politics, momentary sensations and long years of suffering—is the essential property of the human soul." It has a singular uniqueness like the meaning of a sonata that pervades the whole. It is our power of "overcoming death and change and coining meaning out of catastrophes and havoc."[5]

Today the four forms of man are subject to distortions. The proper "molecules" are still ignored and workers are thought of as single atoms whose lives are chopped up into the hours for which they are paid under the factory wage system. There is a despotism of short time spans typical of modern technology, not only in the factory but also for collectives (reduced to election campaigns) and for duals (dissolving love and marriage into a multiplicity of sex experiences). Collectivist solutions are mistakenly sought by revolutionaries to replace the regenerative function of the dual in society. The singular, soul, is either ignored or confused with mind.[6]

Yet though man is multiform, not uniform, the goal and destiny of humankind is unity, like that of a great tree. The worldwide socioeconomy that now exists is new in history and the complete unification of humanity as "the great singular" will be the task of the next millennium (chapter 16). That unity is based on language. "Whoever speaks, believes in the unity of humanity. He believes further that the unity of humanity is evoked by our belief in language."[7]

CHAPTER 4

HUMAN SOULS

AS WE HAVE just seen, the soul is a pervasive unity through which "many bodily states and abundant mental stages become subservient to a specific task of completion." To the soul pertains "all that is connected with the whole duration and form" of a human life: destiny, calling, marriage, name, and other aspects of its entire life history. The forces of the soul carry it through time from birth to death, surviving bodily and mental crises (partial deaths) and thereby attaining its final gestalt, which is only completed when life is over.[1]

A soul is awakened, born, as an answer to being addressed as "you," by the Living God preferably, though answering another god will give it some degree of life. Then it moves rhythmically through phases represented by the other grammatical forms such as "I," "we," and "it" and back to "you" again through its life. Millions of souls remain unborn today, in factories for example, presumably because the divine call does not reach them.[2]

A soul can remain alive and grow only if it preserves the modesty or reticence of a "you," which gives it room for trial and error as it forms its gestalt between fear and hope. Such modesty is destroyed by psychoanalysis today. Growth, change, and conversion are of the soul's essence. When this process ceases, the soul dies. It can die before its body does if it gets stuck in an "I" or "it" phase, e.g. if its character becomes rigidly set or if it merely reacts to external stimuli. It can also be saved from this fate; for example, Schiller's friendship saved Goethe's soul in middle life and Renouvier saved William James's soul from determinism.[3]

The soul is the power in man that overcomes death. The Bible does not teach the immortality of the soul; it teaches "meaningful death, i.e. resurrection." "Death is not overcome in that one does not die, but in that we love each other beyond death." "The central secret of Christianity is in Jesus' power of faith . . . to remain weak and helpless during his life, that he might be loved by each coming generation and thus . . . receive eternal life . . . ."[4]

The Living God and the living soul have much in common. Both are processes. The soul is God's image. Nothing is impossible for God, and the soul achieves the impossible; both create novelty, which seems impossible until afterward. Both are incalculable. Both overcome death. "In every soul a hitherto unknown feature of God enters the world: thus souls reveal God. Without God, no soul; without soul, atheism . . . . The soul is God's step forward in us, by which we separate ourselves from our surrounding world, former world, inner world."[5]

God and soul are of course also to be contrasted. God is the "I" whom the soul answers as "you." "Only He is spirit and we are only souls." Spirit and soul are complementary: inspiration ensouls. "The soul is bride, daughter, mother, but God is father, son, and bridegroom."[6]

Soul is known through experience. The tribal shaman's ecstasy lets his soul leave his body to make room for ancestral spirits who speak through him. Similarly, an actor discovers his own soul reciprocally when the soul spark of the person he is playing induces the same spark in him. All of us believe in the soul through our experience of solidarity with loved ones who die before us.[7]

When psychology is treated as a natural science, it denies the soul because "the soul lives only outside academic lecture halls and laboratories . . . . It is the human being in deadly danger, in lonely origination, when he becomes ecstatic and outgrows mere

analysis, historical community . . . and even poetic transfigura-
tion." Since Descartes, modern thought has tended to identify
soul with mind, conceiving human life as a duality of mind
(thought, consciousness) and body. William James had no use for
the soul and defined psychology as the science of mental processes. Freud at least began the rediscovery of the soul by including
the unconscious "it" as well as the conscious "I" (Descartes'
mind), but he still treated it from the viewpoint of the "I" and
ignored the "you" that is central to the soul. The soul is the
specifically human element in man. It is meant to guide mind and
body and has to fight their resistances. Mind and body, "I" and
"it," are inward and outward configurations of ourselves; soul
enables us to move each way.[8]

Truly scientific knowledge of the soul is attained through the
grammatical method (chapter 1), illustrated in the references to
"you," etc., above. As "the word comes from the soul" and "we
measure the power of language by the way it moves the soul," so
the soul has grammar as its inner structure. "Every turn in the
life of the soul appears as an inflection of its grammatical figure."
Moods and tenses as well as persons are possibilities of the soul.
"Grammatical health" of the soul consists in changing through
the appropriate forms continually. The soul is the "power of
transforming an end into a beginning by obeying a new name."[9]

The grammatical method further relates the soul, as distinctively human, to two other levels above and below it: God and
the world of things. The three levels correspond to "I," "you,"
and "it," as well as to vocative, nominative, and accusative. God
is the power that urges questions on us; man is the being who
answers; the world of things is the subject matter. Any attempt to
reduce these levels to two or one is bound to fail, because they
are present in every breath of life. Treating man as part of the
world, where meaning lies in utility, as something made and not
created, is nihilism.[10]

"Man is the uphill animal of creation." Water flows downhill,
obeying the law of gravity by following the path of least resistance, like nature in general. The human soul can do the seemingly impossible, choosing the path of greatest resistance, overcoming death with new life. The soul is "the rallying point for the
crystallization of all the impossibilities by which we have
conquered the end of the world, the end of our lives, the decay of

our civilization, the agony of our fear, again and again." Through
his soul, man thus participates in his own creation, which God is
continuing throughout history.[11]

CHAPTER 5

SEXES, MARRIAGE,
GENERATIONS

THE TWO SEXES are another multiformity of man, distinctively related to times and spaces as shown below. Of the four forms discussed in chapter 3, the sexes obviously illustrate the dual, which is concerned with propagation. Much of the confusion in theories about sex today is due to the prevalent rationalist individualism, which thinks of people only in the plural or singular, not the dual. Thus, love is perverted into mere sexuality and its time spans reduced from a generation to brief episodes.[1]

"Only both sexes together may be called the image of God," the complete human being. Characteristic masculine traits are active: speaking, doing, creating, penetrating, begetting. Characteristic feminine traits are passive: listening, undergoing, being penetrated, receiving, patiently expecting. The two sexes assume two forms each, which correspond to the four arms of the Cross of Reality: bride, mother, suitor, and possessor.[2]

Among animals, relations between the sexes are instinctively regulated and occur as a matter of course. Not so among humans; sex is the wildest, strongest passion and the state of nature is a state of war between male and female, illustrated by the phenomenon of rape. Hence, it has had to be regulated by law through the institution of marriage and the family, which created islands of peace by establishing a bond between husband and wife and protecting other family relations by incest taboos. Also, thanks to language and the family (made possible by language), parents and children keep in touch, whereas "animals mate and their young forget who their parents were."[3]

Men and women are not exclusively male or female. Through love and family life, they absorb qualities of the opposite sex, thereby becoming mature human beings. In particular, men have natural affinity with the space axis of the Cross of Reality, women with the time axis, being rooted in the past as mothers and expecting the future as brides. Men absorbed something of women's bipolar time sense in the first two millennia of the Christian era, beginning with Jesus and the apostles, who represented the bridelike quality of every soul and the motherliness of the Church, respectively. On the eve of the third millennium, we face the problems of how women can acquire men's space secrets through extremes of inwardness and outwardness. The feminist movement is but a first step, trying to make women like men in the outer world. What women need is affinity with the inward as well as the outward arms of the Cross of Reality and the ability to switch from one to the other.[4]

At the same time, technology has impaired men's acquired time sense and the coming age will have to wrestle over the roots of the right time. Hence, "the first political hour of women has come." World War I completed a process in which humanity sank back from the Christian era into Old Testament times and men thereby lost their ability to transmit the healing, transforming power of the spirit. "The eon of the masculine spirits ends." Woman, the part of creation not used up in the exhausted masculine forms of church and state, is called to give new life to the decaying world of the spirit. "The eternal feminine draws us upward."[5]

Marriage in its traditional form is being undermined by the industrial society produced by technology, which emphasizes the plural at the expense of the dual forms of man (chapter 3). A wedding is considered a private affair, no longer an epoch-making event that alters society. Women are tending to keep their own names rather than adopt their husbands'. Industry has dissolved the household as an economic unit and also involves people in shorter time spans, breaks the spells of longer ones, and thus leads increasingly to divorce. Since marriage was originally instituted by tribes, the revival of tribalism in the third millennium, needed to balance the effects of industrial society, may help strengthen marriage (chapter 16).[6]

The old forms of courtship before marriage have largely disappeared. "It is the great innovation of our time that courtship is becoming a spiritual problem only to be seen and to be solved long after the wedding." "The great adventure of mankind in the present period is women's emancipation . . . . One economy . . . is replacing millions of separate husbandries." "In the old days, a father would never have allowed his daughter to worship Freud, Gandhi, Marx, Bird, or Leslie Howard . . . . Modern women are trying out many deities, many doctrines . . . before they marry." "And only now courtship begins. During the next seven or eight years man and wife seek out their real gods." The couples who find a common faith are unlikely to divorce.[7]

Indeed, sacramental as distinguished from merely legal marriage is a continuing process of transubstantiation for a couple; their marriage is a necessity, not an accident. They form one body that goes on living and keeps growing up through higher stages of the union. Mutual love sees the hidden potentials of each and brings them out. Love or hatred for third parties does not break up the marriage but rejuvenates it. It becomes one life with one biography.[8]

Marriage leads to children and through them to the concatenation of generations that forms human history. "Creative history" does not "begin until at least three or four generations have collaborated toward the same goal." Such linkage does not happen spontaneously; "the hearts of the parents and their children must be turned toward each other, by a special effort," because each generation naturally seeks its own fulfillment according to the spirit of its own time and thus arises a "demonic hatred between fathers and sons." "The Christian era has been one campaign for relating parents and children, the young and the old, in the proper way, again and again."[9]

But today the relationship between the generations has become the most urgent of all questions. Modern technological progress since Descartes, the Enlightenment, and the French Revolution, industry with its fragmentation of time, and then the abyss torn open by two World Wars, have ruptured the generation nexus and have left us with a rebellious generation of "angry young men," while decadent parents have abdicated their role in relation to their children. Sociology must consciously tackle the generation problem today.[10]

CHAPTER 6

FAITH, HOPE, LOVE,
INCARNATION,
AND RESURRECTION

FAITH, HOPE, AND LOVE are inseparable aspects of one time-combining current that connects generations and ages. They are social and spiritual forces, not individual moral virtues. They are "the religious forces of mankind," "the only real motive forces of history and of political life and language." When a soldier risks his life for his country in wartime, faith is the aspect uniting the time before and after his death; the hopes of his country are counting on him; and love welds him and his country together; love is as strong as death. Love unites people in a common present despite the flux of time. Complete faith means "the unshaken acceptance of my own death and of a future without my self," without any idea of what may come. Hope, on the contrary, cares for historical continuity; it projects ideas from the past into the future.[1]

Love must be distinguished from sexuality. It is not a form of desire or of will. It is not self-assertive but self-forgetful: "Man has love lest his self imprison his soul." Love is a combination of sacrifice and "the power of yearning which transforms us."

25

"Abraham Lincoln is the everlasting hero of self-forgetful devotion . . . ."[2]

Likewise, faith and hope are not matters of will. I cannot will to hope or will to believe, despite William James. "James's 'will to believe' ushered in the revolt of the masses, because it withdrew the prop from our faith in God: God's faith in Man." Faith covers all our experiences of being created, being in God's melting pot. "Faith opens itself to presentiments yet unknown to it." Hope, on the other hand, is the "agreeable expectation of our own wishes, of what is already known as agreeable." The four gospels scarcely use the word "hope" because they bring a new faith. Jesus triumphed by faith alone, without hope. Only thereafter could his followers hope to have faith like him.[3]

"Our faith in forces greater than man's intelligence, a charity greater than any social intelligence ever warrants, and unbending hope in the victory over the worst fiend, animate those who by their personal decisions and sacrifices enable . . . us to cooperate and to live inside of some semblance of order." "Faith, hope and love . . . connect you with the day of creation and the Judgment Day, because faith brings in all that has still to be created and hope holds on to anything God already has created and you would like to see repeated and renewed. The balance between the two is charity, is love. And this love enables the person inside yourself to do justice to your own past as well as to the future." ". . . faith, love and hope are one trinitarian stream. We believe in the triune God for this very reason . . . ." "The presence of God, i.e. the working of love, faith, and hope, is the condition of our existence through time." "Thanks to hope, faith, and love, we are members of the whole length of history from beginning to end." They create human solidarity, enable humans to say "we."[4]

Though faith, hope, and love are spiritual forces, they build *bodies* of time and they lead to the *incarnation* of the soul. Why is embodiment or incarnation important? Why must the Word become flesh? Why believe in the resurrection of the body? Why does materializing matter? To materialize is to be realized, become real, come true.[5]

Descartes, Kant, and modern idealist philosophies separated mind and body to the disparagement of the latter. The Greeks held that the incorporeal is better than bodies. But ideas and ideals have to be lived, embodied, not merely thought. Greek ideas remained ideas in antiquity, changed no institutions, but "in the Christian era all spirit is spirit-become-flesh." Even Marxism became a mass movement.[6]

Descartes and Kant separated mind and body because they ignored the role of language. Language is not a mere tool of minds. It is "a field of energy . . . in which a human receives or loses his mind, changes or hardens it." Language connects minds and bodies instead of separating them. Speaking and listening involve complex physical and physiological processes. Hence, the grammatical method (chapter 1) calls for *leibhaftige Grammatik*, corporeal grammar. It further shows how language creates social relations, incorporating people into social bodies such as army, church, or clan, and thus "word becomes flesh."[7]

The resurrection of the body is one of the laws of men's creation in history. "A new soul, a fresh originality of the human heart, thereby survives the man or nation in which it came to birth and incarnates itself in a spiritual succession of typical representatives through the ages." St. Francis, for example, died without offspring, but Franciscan humanity has flourished ever since, and not only in his Order." "When Abraham Lincoln walked into Richmond on foot in 1865, St. Francis had conquered the powers of this earth." "Here, ruler and servant were blended into one." It was not conscious imitation, but genuine succession. "In like fashion, Christian astronomers, chemists, doctors, preachers, missionaries, painters, masons have populated the earth. Anticipating a Last Judgment over our corruptible flesh, they have come into the flesh out of the spirit, achieving a tempestuous resurrection from the dead in the name of the new life." Christ rose again in his disciples and the Church, which became his second body. "We, all the faithful, constitute Christ in our own time."[8]

CHAPTER 7

TIME, SPACES, WHOLES

MULTIFORMITY HOLDS not only for man but for times and spaces. Philosophers often speak of space and time, or space-time, in the singular, but these are false singulars, false because they do not correspond to actual human experience. They are admissible only as abstractions of modern physics, legitimate for that field but not beyond it. They are uniform, whereas human times and spaces are multiform. History moves rhythmically, not mechanically. The Cross of Reality (chapter 1), with its two temporal and two spatial fronts, is the foundation of that multiformity, and grammar is "the philosophy of times and spaces."[1]

Our experiences of times and of spaces move in opposite directions. Time is a flux of moments to begin with, but as a gift of human society through language we learn to bind them into longer periods: days, weeks, years, and so on. Our highest achievement would be to unite all into a single history of humankind, from Adam to Judgment Day. That would be the greatest example of the power over time that we are challenged to achieve in the third millennium A.D. (chapter 16). Space, on the other hand, seems

28

boundless and undivided to begin with, when an infant stretches out its arms from the cradle. Society and language lead us to experience more and more boundaries, delimit more spaces, and also to separate inner from outer spaces. When people talk together, an inner space is created. "The smallest inner space, where two or three are gathered together, is the grandest space."[2]

The second millennium, "the space millennium" (chapter 15), has been marked by "the predominance of spaces" against which the third millennium is to rise. Descartes, for example, "put time into space, made time at its best a fourth dimension of space." On the contrary, "spaces are fourth dimensions of each particular time-space. To every time-space belong future, past, and a now, and thanks to the fourth dimension of space the moment of now widens into a cheerful present." "Spaces are just developed time-spaces. No space has emerged by itself among realities, but only at a time-point." "Time is more essential for us than space." ". . . man is peculiarly a temporal being, ever but an exile and a pilgrim in the world of space." The priority of time is rooted in the process of speaking and the three tenses of grammar and is therefore basic for speech thinkers. "Spaces are projected times." The European revolutions (chapter 15) started without reference to space and then took root in a particular soil.[3]

In getting away from the predominance of spaces, nothing is more important than restoring men's sense of timing, which space obsession has impaired. "When?" is "the question of all questions of our time." ". . . every human being, for his own salvation, must be trained in the timing of all his experiences throughout life. Especially must he learn to fear being 'too early' and 'too late' as the greatest of sins." ". . . true presence of mind, the power to live in the fullness of time, is something that has to be won arduously and preserved by perpetual vigilance." "The moment not 'seized by the forelock' avenges itself on us for the rest of our life."[4]

The most striking difference between the dead time of Newton or Einstein (moving uniformly in one direction) and experienced living time is that the latter is bipolar and involves movement in two directions, toward past and toward future, and the tension between them yields a present. In the nature described by physics, there is no present, merely a cut in the time line like the edge of a razor. The human present is an overlap between the encroaching future and the still-lasting past, where society through speech creates an inner space. That occurs only in peace; in war, enemies do not speak and there is no present, only past and future. Events in physics are strictly determined by the past, but the human present is free to change, grow, be redetermined between past and future, and God's presence distinguishes the Living God from blind fate. "Future means novelty, surprise; it means outgrowing past habits and attainments."[5]

The contrast between living time and dead time can be expanded into a spectrum of times, which exhibits at least five degrees of aliveness, counting the zero of dead time. Each higher sphere except the first is more alive than the next lower and each is more dead than the next higher. One can discriminate more than five, but the five are irreducible, like colors in the spectrum of light. The five can be described in many ways, for example: mechanical, organic, conscious, passionate, calamitous-redeeming; technology, culture, science, art, religion; death, sleep, work, love, new name (old name destroyed); resistance, rhythm, acceleration, perpetuation, creation. We need all spheres, but none of us can embody all at the same time. Hence, we keep shifting between them and we need other people to supplement our lacks. That is why the spectrum of times is the chief instrument of sociology and why sociology aims at "the fullness of all the times" (*Vollzahl der Zeiten*), which constitutes supreme happiness, "the harmony of the spheres."[6]

Another multiformity of times is found in the three times of human life: childhood, adulthood, and elderhood. Each is subject to four "commands of maturation" which together form a twelve-tone scale, each tone a key to whole-time (*Ganzzeit*). The three times are periods in which inspiration moves into us from the past, works in us during the present, and then is transmitted by us into the future. The twelve commands are: for childhood, obey, read, learn, sing; for adulthood, doubt, analyze, protest, persevere; and for elderhood, govern, teach, prophesy, and bequeath. Each prepares for the next, and the last is the most important of all. Thus, old age, the stage of elders or priests, should be given a crowning role in life, rather than being pitied or ignored as it has tended to be in recent times. The secret of elderhood "lies in the fact that an old man is through with his own life but not at all through with life . . . . He is . . . the guardian of life's continuity . . . . he is peculiarly the regenerative force in society; he sees to it that the full cycle of life is re-begun in the proper order." Today's "secular" psychology reverses the proper order of importance and expects the child to "pull itself up by its own bootstraps and become itself, express itself, live by itself."[7]

God's relationship to times and spaces differs from that of humans and also from that of gods. He is not in space; He creates spaces. He is pure time, *actus purissimus* as the Scholastics called Him, and His time *is* singular, one, perpetual, eternal. His eternity should not be thought of as an endless line or as sheer timelessness; He ends epochs and creates new ones. Eternity does not mean "world without end." World after world ends but Christ, "the Lord of the eons," goes through them all, linking them together perpetually. Miracles are not exceptions made by the Eternal in the spatial mechanism of the world. "The form of every little eternity rests in the overlapping Great Eternity as its miracle."[8]

Such is the "full eternity" of "eons of eons," but an epoch is a "short eternity." Epochs are wholes. "Epochs are not atoms out of which history puts itself together. Rather they are rungs of a ladder on which the Holy Spirit descends into the world." ". . . whereas in space we put together a whole out of parts . . . in time a whole articulates itself. And it does so in that it enters us as its branches and leaves." "Wholes carry history." The transition from tribe to cosmic empire (chapter 9) was not a gradual evolution but a change from one whole to another. The rhythmic correspondence of the European revolutions (chapter 15) shows them taking place within a whole, an economy of forces that reaches across the centuries.[9]

TWO

HISTORICAL
PERSPECTIVES

CHAPTER 8

HUMAN LIFE
BEGAN WITH TRIBES

THIS CHAPTER DEALS with the tribe as the earliest distinctively human way of life, not its subsequent modification through mixture with later forms, or its fragmentation or degeneration.[1]

"The direction of love is the decisive power of history," and tribes were generated by love of the living for the dead. Animals mate and their young forget who their parents were. Animals do not know of death or of their forebears and descendants. They die alone and are not buried by other animals. Human life began with tribes, who did bury their dead and mourned them. In this way, death enters subsequent life. The young become successors of the old and inherit their function. "'The dead look at the living' is the basic law of the tribal constitution." The dead look at the living from the totem pole and their spirits speak to the living through the shaman's mask. Formal, name-using language, first created by the tribes, makes this possible; the body is buried but the dead hero can still be identified by name when his spirit enters the shaman and speaks through the mask to the listening tribal assembly. The dead are considered still alive, the past not past. The tribe is thus based on a lie and its future has to pay for it.[2]

The tribe's Cross of Reality is thus dominated by the past. Everything is sacrificed for the past. The spirits of the ancestors govern. They are highly suspicious of youth and oppose all change. The future arm of the Cross of Reality is represented by the stone altar on which innovators are sacrificed—the widespread sacrifice of the firstborn child is an expression of this attitude. The inner arm is represented by the dancing-ground where marriages are made in the name of the ancestral spirits, and by the resulting families, created by the tribe to be islands of peace between the sexes, protected by incest taboos. The outer arm is represented by the warpath, pursued against bush and jungle by huntsmen and against enemies by the warriors (all the men of the tribe) under orders from the spirits. Hence endless blood feuds are driven onward by spirits of ancestors who were killed or insulted. Most tribes have perished from excesses of such "inspiration."[3]

The past-oriented reality of the ancient tribe, however, was only half of its existence, the half of which it thought and spoke. The other half was its unspoken drive to migrate. Tribes scattered over the whole earth and degenerated when they ceased to move on. The "all" in which they ventured was uncanny to them, and they kept moving out of dread of attack from one or another direction. But through this movement their future came upon them. It enabled them to slough off excesses of the magic by which they sought to project their own rites over the chaos of the surrounding world and which tended to petrify their lives.[4]

Though the tribe was consciously governed by the past, it was not a very long past. Tribal memory extended back only five or six generations. Thus, their short memory made them like a "time raft" floating down the stream of time. If the raft was broken, e.g. if the enemy got its totem pole, the tribe no longer existed.[5]

In addition to burial and marriage, the tribe instituted a third miracle in human history, the right to hospitality on the part of strangers, even enemies. In this respect, it anticipated both the miracle of Pentecost, when the Holy Spirit overcame the vengeful ancestral spirits, and our task today, the peaceful unification of the whole human race.[6]

CHAPTER 9

COSMIC EMPIRES

WHILE TRIBES CONTINUED to exist, new ways of human life arose in Egypt and Mesopotamia and later in India, China, and Latin America (Aztec, Maya, Inca). They will be called cosmic empires (or empires for short) because they were oriented toward the stars and were ruled by "cosmocrats" such as Pharaoh. This chapter will deal primarily with Egypt because it is the clearest example of the new form, as well as one of the oldest.[1]

Flood legends preserve the memory of the sudden shift from tribe to empire. Migrating tribes encountered flooded rivers, e.g. the Nile. Baffled, they looked at each other and lifted their eyes and their love to the heavens instead of to the ancestors. In this way, they were able to make peace and settle down, instead of fighting and migrating, to organize a huge territory with a large population (the stars being the same for all), to calculate the regular periods of flooding, and to cultivate the rich floodlands between floods. Instead of the dead speaking to the living, the empire's constitution was based on heaven speaking to earth.[2]

Death was not so much denied as bypassed by climbing to the sky. The sun and stars set and rose, each year followed a regular calendar which the empire developed, and time moved in longer cycles of eternal recurrence. Egyptian astrologers calculated that the same pattern of constellations would recur every "great year" (once every 1,460 years), and it did. There were no real endings or genuine beginnings, no novelty, no true future. The time axis of the empire's Cross of Reality was stunted into a kind of eternal present. Empires gave to space what they stole from time; they had a space delusion; they turned times into spaces.[3]

Further contrasts with tribal traits throw cosmic empires into relief. Empires felt no urge to migrate because they were no longer terrified by the "all"; they lived in an orderly cosmos. Thus, they settled in one territory, developed intensive agriculture, built enormous buildings of stone (notably temples and pyramids) with the vast labor supplies available in flood season. The stone and the lavish use of gold and jewels were symbols of the eternity in which they lived. The family of gods ordered the cosmos in its regular patterns, and Pharaoh was himself a god, obeyed accordingly. People fell prostrate before him. Pharaohs often married their sisters, breaking the tribal incest taboo. Instead of making graves for their fathers, they built their own tombs or pyramids, plundering those of their predecessors. Even the names of their fathers were concealed. They commanded living judges to judge the dead, whereas in tribes the dead judged the living. Tribes were warlike democracies of warriors who were constantly mobilized; empires were peaceful and developed a hierarchy of classes and an elaborate specialization of occupations ordered from the top down by the "pope-emperor." In place of tattooing human bodies, empires wrote inscriptions (really prescriptions) on temples, using magic hieroglyphs or similar writing to conjure the gods.[4]

The era of empires is over. An emperor claimed to bring heavenly order down to his empire on earth, where he was the center. Today, the earth is seen as a planet, itself part of the cosmic order, and no point on it can be central. But man's being called into the universe must not be lost. The chaotic tribal "all" must not return. The system of cosmic reference can be expressed in other than empire ways. And, as it was for Pharaoh, the political ordering of human life will still be a matter of faith, not a fact of nature.[5]

CHAPTER 10

THE CHOSEN PEOPLE
OF THE COMING GOD: ISRAEL

A THIRD WAY of life arose with the Jews, beginning with Abraham and continuing through Moses, the prophets, and the diaspora down to the present day. When Abraham left the land of his birth and waited for God to fulfill His promises, he began the permanent function that the Jews have represented in history: exile and waiting. Moses continued it with the exodus from Egypt and the journey toward the promised land. As the tribe was oriented toward the past, the cosmic empire toward the present, Israel was oriented toward the future. That was the new direction of its love—toward the one Living God, the ever-coming God. Israel was chosen by Him as a living sacrifice, to perform its function of exile and waiting, bearing witness to Him.[1]

Further contrasts with tribe and empire throw Israel into relief. The institution of the Sabbath as a day of rest took people out of the restless domination of ancestral spirits or recurring constellations, to rest in their Creator. For the tribe, only the spirit of the dead hero could say "I," speak as an independent person; the tribesmen only responded as an answering chorus. For the empire, only the gods addressed Pharaoh as "Thou," treating him as one of them; the people were slaves who fell on their faces before him. But Israel is a "We-people" of persons; each can speak frankly and converse. The empire brought heaven to earth; Israel's God created the heavens *and* the earth. Flood legends recalled the empires' break with tribal ritual; the single event of Noah surviving the flood records Israel's break with the empires' liturgy of recurrent floods—every act of the Living God is unique and unpredictable, like his subsequent rainbow. Moses or his predecessor invented a script that replaced the tribal tattoo as well as the magic Egyptian hieroglyphs; thus, he could write the Ten Commandments without involving tribe or empire. Other contrasts with tribalism were: the serpent as tempter in the Garden of Eden replacing the dependence of tribes on animals, e.g. for trails; Abraham's not slaying Isaac and hence not becoming a tribal chief through sacrificing his firstborn; Moses' grave unknown. The laws given Israel, including dietary laws, served to protect it from tribes' and empires' influence. Israel achieved a different attitude toward death, not denying it like the tribe or ignoring it like the empire but discounting it like the passing of all visible things while waiting for God's future coming as Messiah.[2]

The period that came after Moses and the wilderness was indeed a resorption of some aspects of the empire: land was settled, kings ruled, and the temple was built. But the prophet Nathan could rebuke King David in the name of Jahveh. The census—administrative device of empires—was forbidden. And the Hebrew scriptures were written, permitting God's spoken word to run on through the ages. These three points were the pillars of the constitution of Israel's state-of-the-future, enabling Israel to remain Israel. Solomon's temple was different from the temples of Egypt, not being a limited space mirroring heaven but radiating unbounded influence, corresponding to the one infinite God instead of the many gods of Egypt.[3]

With their scripture, the Jews created history in the proper sense. Pagan rulers had to appear, and claim to be, infallible. The Bible shows how man proposes and God disposes; human beings have their aims and programs, but God decides what takes effect. Such is the moral disarmament of the Bible. The Jew can admit his weakness. That is his strength. Being powerless in the hands of God is the essence of Israel's story.[4]

"Israel voided the Temple ... the rites ... the arts. In these three acts she emptied the three great 'speeches' of the heathen, the tribal, the templar, and the artistic, of their lure .... But Israel recognized herself in the divine 'No' spoken over man's naive pretenses. Majestically, the Bible is based on three divine 'No's' ... Man's Fall ... the Great Flood ... the Exodus .... 'Revelation' is a knowledge of God's will, after his 'No' to our will has become known. Only then is God pure future, pure act—only when all his former creations stand exposed as nongods .... On this basis the Jews became prayer. Israel is neither a nation nor a state nor a race, but it *is* prayer."[5]

CHAPTER 11

THE ANCIENT GREEKS

THE FOURTH DISTINCTIVE way of life created in the ancient world came with the Greeks during the late second millennium and the first millennium B.C. When Hellenes, Achaeans, and other tribes migrated south, they encountered settled peoples following a cosmic empire way of life, notably in Thessaly and Mycenae; and they came to the sea. There resulted a mixture of tribal and imperial ways of life, but one so original as to put it on a par with tribe, empire, and Israel. As the tribes settled, they formed city-states one at a time over many, many years, and these in turn founded others as colonies, scattered over the islands of the Mediterranean and parts of Italy and Asia Minor. Each time a vital decision had to be made at once as to what tribal and what imperial elements were to be combined in a given city. But the whole Greek world was also a unity, sharing the gods of Mount Olympus and the seagoing life, in which the Argonauts were pioneers. Thus, for the first time in history spiritual boundaries no longer coincided with political ones; the sea united the Greek cosmos, and a Greek learned to look at all political units including his own from outside, from the ship's deck, as objects which his mind could compare. This was the world which Homer united through his song.[1]

Comparison led to generalization. The pluralism of Greek life, with its many cities and many myths, gave rise to poetry that embraced them all (Homer and the tragedians), then philosophy, then the philology of the Alexandrian Encyclopedists. The Greeks thus discovered the life of the mind, of liberal arts and sciences inspired by the muses, the free realm of ideas, as a way of finding unity outside political pluralism. Such was the essence of Greek humanism, enabling men of different political groups to recognize each other as human, as did Achilles and Priam in the *Iliad*.[2]

But if humanism was in that way a blessing, it was also a curse. It came to regard the universal as better, more beautiful and true, than the particular; rest as better than motion. Parmenides condemned the real world as mere appearance. Plato turned the gods into abstract ideas, names into concepts. The Greek cult of the intellect developed as the gods died, and it was based on dread of being transformed. Humanism achieves mutual recognition in space but it misjudges the times of history. It deals in abstract generalizations, whereas only the particular can govern, be determinant. In place of the "I" behind the tribal mask, the "Thou" with which Pharaoh was embraced by the gods, and the "we" of God's people, the humanist uses the third person "it" to neutralize human history by speaking in generalities about "a god," "a rite," etc.[3]

The ideal world of the Greek humanist represented another attitude toward time and death. We have seen that tribe, empire, and chosen people embodied three modes of time: past, present, and future. They seemed inhumanly inaccessible to each other, in unavoidable exterminating conflict. But the Greeks did the impossible—they created a way of evading the conflict by appealing to the spare time, play time, leisure of a theater-going, school-attending, games-watching public. This gave the Greek spirit a permanent place in human history. They developed the arts and sciences, mathematics and physics, poetry and philosophy, the Olympic and other games, as indispensable elements of education. Plato, Aristotle, Stoics, and Epicureans formed schools. The Greek evasion led into a divine world apart from the real world. In it the dependence of life on suffering and death could be forgotten by a spectator public composed of detached individuals who felt no duties to gods or men.[4]

The ideal world did not affect the real world in ancient Greece. "The Greeks changed neither tribe nor empire. No idol was ever given up by any people thanks to Greek philosophy. Ideas did not change the world in antiquity; they do that in our era." Yet without realizing it, the Greeks did perform a historical function beyond themselves by connecting the older empires of Asia Minor and Egypt with the subsequent Roman Empire, which in turn became a framework for Christendom and the Holy Roman Empire.[5]

CHAPTER 12

JESUS CHRIST
THE CENTER OF HISTORY

AS WE HAVE SEEN, four modes of time were realized in human history before Christ. They were past-oriented, present-oriented, future-oriented, and free time for the arts and sciences. They were realized through four streams of language in four ways of life with four attitudes toward death: tribe, cosmic empire, chosen people, and Greece. All these existed together when Jesus was born and a man seemed to need all four for a complete life, but each claimed exclusive validity. The result was a shambles.[1]

"Because he was the first to turn mankind's direction toward unity, Jesus is the center of history." He "placed himself at the source of the times, the heart point, from which we may come ever again to the formation of tribes, empires, humanists, and the true Israel." Thus, he made the fullness of all the times (*vollzahl der Zeiten*) available to humanity. He became the center of history by living the law that humans can progress from fragmentariness to completeness only by surviving the death of old allegiances and beginning new ones. Thus, he was the first perfect human because he made this process the theme of his whole life and made others follow him in this process. They follow him because he did not seek personal success in his own lifetime but founded the Church instead, thereby becoming the most successful man in history.[2]

Jesus was the first to be independent of all the times, free to enter or leave them.[3] He was the watershed of history, bequeathing the whole future to us because he inherited the whole past.[4] Having proved himself free from the authority of the four streams of language, he "became the founder of a new language in which they are all merged in a new beginning," "a new dimension of language in which all human generations are brothers."[5] The central place in the history of language thus belongs to him too. "He saved the straying gentiles and the locked-up Jews ... by cross-fertilizing the four paths of speech." He was "the Noon of our history."[6]

Jesus achieved the climax in human dealing with death. The tribes denied death; their ancestors spoke to the living through the shaman's mask. The empires detoured death with temples and pyramids reflecting the cosmic order of the stars. The Jews gave death only a negative significance, something to be endured while awaiting the Messiah. The leisured Greek public could forget death in artistic and philosophic contemplation. Through the crucifixion and resurrection of Christ, "death was included as a positive factor within life" and was thus overcome, becoming the gateway to new life.[7]

"As the center of history, Jesus can" also "be seen to unite Buddha, Lao-tse, and Abraham around the Cross of Reality." The latter three had created "zero situations" to help people avoid getting stuck on each of the four fronts of the Cross: Buddha by negating the strife on the outer front, Lao-tse by turning from the perpetual functioning of Confucian Chinese society to nonfunctioning on the inner front, Abraham for the backward and forward fronts by his exodus from Ur and by waiting for God to fulfill his promises. But "whereas the Jews identified end and beginning in God and virtually ignored everything in between, Jesus created a historical process in which ... every present is equally immediate to God." "Jesus embedded all times, including his own, in one supertime, one eternal present ... and thereby the Cross of Reality was completed. We now gained full freedom toward all trends."[8]

CHAPTER 13

THE CHRISTIAN ERA

THE CHRISTIAN ERA does not include everything A.D. The last Chinese emperor, for example, died in 1911, yet he represented a pre-Christian form of life, as did the German princes until their overthrow in 1919.[1] The Christian era includes only those lives affected by Christianity, and even for them it is always possible to backslide and fall out of the Christian era.[2] Indeed, Christianity itself has known periods of bankruptcy, as in the tenth and fifteenth centuries, yet emerged reborn, and it is bankrupt again today. It does not abolish but overcomes death.[3]

We secede from the Christian era when we believe, with Spengler for example, that history runs in repetitive cycles.[4] Christianity brings freedom from these and other pagan traits, permitting the in-break of novelty, progress, true future, as we participate in the further creation of humanity.[5] "Precisely because Christianity created future, progress is the gift of the Christian era, and it vanishes in proportion as we secede from that era."[6] Christianity creates future through its faith in death and resurrection, "the power that enables us to die to our old habits and ideals . . . and take the first step into a genuine future."[7]

There are no sacral languages in the Christian era, as there

47

were for tribes, empires (e.g. Egyptian hieroglyphs), and Hebrews. No Christian now speaks the language Jesus spoke. The gospels are in Greek, the Western Church used Latin, and the Bible has been translated into more than a thousand languages.[8] "All nations of the Christian age are plurilingual," as Latin served Germany and others, and "the task of our era is the mutual opening of languages."[9] Names may start in one language, but they are capable of entering all, forming a universal language of names, and Jesus brought "the conscious institution of the universal language of names in his name."[10]

Thus, the Christian era is "the self-conscious period of mankind during which man is making a purposeful effort toward unity and universality." "The meaning of the Christian era is that the time of divided loyalties is coming to an end . . . . In every epoch after Christ another part of creation is finding its home in lasting unity." "The story of salvation on earth is the advance of the singular against the plural . . . one God, one world, one humankind."[11]

The Christian era is accordingly divided into three periods of roughly a thousand years each. In the first millennium, the main interest lies in the conversion of *pre-Christians* from many gods to *one* God by the Church. In the second, the main interest lies in *co-Christian* affairs: the Papacy as a worldly power, the territorial states in competition with the Church, the sciences establishing the unity of *one* world of nature. In the third millennium, the main interest will lie in "the *post-Christians*, the members of the family of Christ simply building further on the deed of the cross," creating *one* human society. For them, neither Church nor state are the chief concern. Thus, Church, state, and society (*Gesellschaft*) are the three gestalts of the Christian era.[12]

CHAPTER 14

THE FIRST MILLENNIUM
OF THE CHRISTIAN ERA:
THE CHURCH

THE THEME OF the first millennium is "God and the soul," the "liberation of souls" from times and spaces of the world through conversion to faith in God. "The epoch begins with the incarnation of the sound, the healed soul. It ends with the institution of the Feast of All Souls (A.D. 998)." "The Church is the healed soul of our race writ large." "The feast of All Saints, instituted in the ninth century, is the expression of its perfected self-awareness." The names of the saints compose in mosaic the likeness of God—man created in God's image. The Church reveals to the soul its law, to love that which is hardest, thereby overcoming death and achieving something definitive, once for all.[1]

Thus, "the Church is the immense achievement of the first millennium"—its formation as the first all-human institution and its growth by converting pre-Christians.[2] The task of the Church was to perpetuate what Jesus began, placing death before life. "The ability to look death in the face, and the greater ability to live again and further with death behind: these two contradictory abilities had first of all to be embodied as a power within the powers of transience." The Church became "an unending times womb" through which we are "shifted before, after, in and out of our own time" and are free to enter and leave all times.[3]

The Church consisted of four acts of implanting death before life: mass, mission, communion, and asceticism. In the mass, the Church reached back to its origin, the deed of Christ on the cross. Through mission, leading to the conversion of pre-Christians, the Church moved forward into the future. By communion, the Lord's Supper, the Church created a community of people who may not belong together otherwise, but who through the death of their own will experience a common will, a "within." By asceticism, the Church expressed hostility toward the outer world and its rationalist secularism. This was typified by the rise of monasticism, but every Christian must abstain from the part of the world that is sinful and worthy of death.[4]

With the conversion of Constantine, a major change occurred for the Church. After centuries of persecution, it then came in danger of absorption by the Roman Empire, which would have meant the end of Christianity. Four great saints prevented this. St. Anthony, a generation before Constantine, chose to live in the wilderness instead of the fertile land of Egypt, thus preserving the spirit of superiority toward the world, as did the monks who followed in his footsteps, forestalling any reconciliation of Church and world. St. Athanasius, by fighting the Arians and supporting the Council of Nicaea, which established the divinity of Christ in the Creed, made it impossible for the "godlike" emperor to be confused with Christ. St. Jerome was the first monk to do work, in his case the mental work of translating the Bible, thus leading monasteries to hand down the literature and science of the past independent of any worldly empire. After Rome had fallen, these treasures were preserved by Irish monks. St. Augustine in his *City of God* made the human soul the carrier of one history in which God is creating his kingdom, outlasting not only Rome but all others.[5]

Augustine was the last great individual convert to Christianity. After Rome in the West was overrun by northern tribes, whole peoples were baptized together but without dissolving tribal ties. In earlier centuries, pagan city life had furnished atomized individuals, despairing sick souls who were ripe for conversion by the Church and with which it could then build its spiritual order, forming new ties. Now an externally Christianized world remained largely pagan within, and the year 1000 A.D. was the most pre-Christian time since the birth of Christ; only the clergy were Christian.[6]

The second half of the first millennium witnessed two other major events, the threat of Islam and the schism between the Roman Catholic and Greek Orthodox churches. The barbarian Christians of the north, notably the Franks, forced the pope into the change in the Creed that caused the schism, but they also fought off Islam.[7]

CHAPTER 15

THE SECOND MILLENNIUM:
WORLD REVOLUTIONS

WHEREAS THE FIRST millennium was primarily Church history, the second has been primarily "world" history in a special sense—not a history *of* the world, but the story of men's dealings *with* the world. The Church made men indifferent to the world and turned their eyes to God. The second millennium looks "with God's eyes on a world that has become indifferent." The Greek cosmos contained gods and souls, and the territories of ancient empires were sacrosanct, but by the second millennium, the world had become profane; hence, men were free to change it, manipulate it. The world is not an object of faith or love, only of hope for what we can make of it. We are in God's place in relation to it. Thus, a new relationship to the world has been the historic achievement of the second millennium.[1]

World history is peculiarly a history of world revolutions whose "circumvolution" rounds out the millennium. There were revolutions of sorts in antiquity and there will be in the third millennium, but not world revolutions. The latter are total; they influence the world, not just the country where they occur; they adapt to each other and learn to coexist, yielding a cumulative result.[2] World history consists of revolutions because as we work on the world, we become enslaved by what we create, leading to another revolution and the next enslavement.[3] The revolution in each case breaks out where the enslavement by the old order is most acutely felt, most troublesome, and revolutionaries act in desperation. This point of sorest pressure leads all preparatory factors to work together toward revolution.[4]

The pressure point leading to the first revolution was supplied by the Holy Roman emperors from Otto I to Henry III, who wielded authority over the Church (which had by then degenerated, especially in Rome) and reformed it. This culminated in the Synod of Sutri, 1046 A.D., when the emperor deposed three rival popes and installed one of his own choosing. That led to the revolution of the pope against the emperor, thereby unleashing the whole cycle of revolutions occupying the second millennium. The pope was able to make his revolution stick in the end because the emperor's power did not extend over all the West and the pope's influence did. Thus, the pope proved the better unifier and established his own control of the Church in place of the emperor's.[5]

Important background for the Papal Revolution came also from the Monastery of Cluny. Its abbot, Odilo, inaugurated the Feast of All Souls; monks prayed for *all* souls from the beginning of the world to its end, thereby beginning "world" history because their prayers concerned the whole world. "In anticipating the lessons of death, Europe learned democracy, she learned unity, she learned universality. All Souls is the cornerstone of all our modern civilization." Also, by organizing and administering from Cluny a whole group of affiliated monasteries over the empire, Odilo was the first to establish a translocal corporation.[6]

The first revolutionary pope, Gregory VII, made himself "monk-emperor," fusing the translocal functions of Cluny and of the emperor, who was the judge of this world. Gregory sought power that would be both centralized and universal, whereas the bishop of Rome had had no real power over other bishops and was at best primary because he held the See of St. Peter.[7] Gregory's decision was recorded in the *Dictatus papae*, a document he dictated in 1075 A.D. It actually began the revolution, though carrying it out was a task that ran through a series of popes, with many ups and downs. Crusades for capturing the Holy Sepulcher in Jerusalem, preached by the revolutionary popes, united the West in a way that emperors never could.[8] After Gregory VII, two sovereign powers, pope and emperor, balanced each other, a political dualism that was the secret of European freedom.[9]

With the Concordat of Worms in 1122, years after Gregory's death, the revolution culminated in a way that gave the papacy less than Gregory had claimed but a necessary minimum. He had claimed the right to choose all bishops. The Concordat gave the Church that right outside Germany. But with that much power, the pope could build his own clergy under his centralized authority.[10]

The Concordat of Worms was followed by a period of papal arrogance (1122–57), including a Crusade that failed, and then a period of humiliation (1158–98) in which the results of the revolution were put to the test of great hardships, such as the loss of Jerusalem, which had been won by the first Crusade.[11]

With Pope Innocent III, however, a new period began. In that it continued the rivalry of pope and emperor, it was the second half of the Papal Revolution, but it was also the Guelphic or Italian Revolution, in which Guelphs supported by the pope struggled against Ghibellines, partisans of the emperor, to make Italy independent. These were the "clerical revolutions" that occupied the first half of the second millennium.[12]

Following the period of papal humiliation mentioned above, Innocent III made a fresh start in the struggle with the emperor when he read his new revolutionary document, *Deliberatio de statu imperii*, before a consistory of cardinals in 1200. It debated the claims of three candidates for the vacant imperial throne and concluded in favor of the Guelphic one. By this time, the emperor controlled almost all of Italy plus Sicily, thus having a stranglehold on the Papacy. Innocent sought to recoup as papal states the territories around Rome that had been gathered by the Church over many centuries and to eliminate imperial control of the south. Finally, with the execution of Conradin, the last of the Hohenstaufen emperors, by Charles of Anjou in 1268, the papal aim was accomplished and no emperor again dominated the Italian peninsula.[13]

The Italian Revolution, occupying the same period and pursuing similar aims, arose from the fact that the cities of northern and southern Italy were treated more like conquered territories than as part of the empire. They did not participate in electing the emperors, and emperors had been chosen from all the major German tribes but none from Italy. The territories between the Alps and Rome were treated as mere way stations for the emperors and their armies who came from Germany to Rome eighty-five times between 950 and 1250. When the emperor destroyed Milan in 1161, that became the pressure point, the last straw that made revolution inevitable.[14]

St. Francis of Assisi was the man who linked together the Papal and Italian revolutions. He supported the Papacy instead of attacking its worldly wealth as previous "poverty" movements had done. The pope visited Francis on his deathbed and canonized him in 1228. The Franciscan and also the Dominican friars grew roots among the city people instead of living in isolated country monasteries, and they set up an effective peace movement which countered the tendency of the many city-states to go to war with each other. Thus the Italians were able to work together in alliance with the Papacy to become independent of the emperor.[15]

After the death of Conradin, the Papacy went through another period of arrogance and then another of humiliation during the exile in Avignon (1309–77). Thereafter, the college of cardinals was unable to take unified action in choosing popes, running the Church without a pope at times, and the Church fell back on a series of councils for guidance. Finally, for the last half of the fifteenth century, the pope settled again in Rome, and Italy enjoyed its golden age of the Renaissance, while troubles elsewhere mounted toward the next revolution.[16]

The German Reformation began the series of "secular revolutions" which occupied the second half of the second millennium. Several factors led up to it. Its pressure point came in 1415 at the Council of Constance, when Emperor Sigismund broke his promises of safe conduct to John Hus and burned him at the stake after he was condemned as a heretic by the Council. That led to the terrible Hussite wars, which lasted fifty years. Thereafter, the Germans had little faith in councils or patience with the burning of heretics. In 1512, another emperor, Maximilian, tried to become pope himself, which would have combined the two offices that had been balancing each other since the Papal Revolution. If the emperor no longer saw himself as polar opposite to the pope, the time was ripe for a revolution against the pope.[17]

Germany was at a great disadvantage in Church councils, having only thirty-five bishops as against the Italians' three hundred. Moreover, Luther's prince, the elector of Saxony, had to deal with a number of dioceses that held jurisdiction over parts of his territory but reached beyond it, a ready source of conflict between ecclesiastical and secular authority. Also, a hundred monasteries occupied a third of Germany tax-free and lived under "religions" of their own, granted by the pope. These features illustrate the maxim that a revolution breaks out in the most backward area, the one where conditions differ most from those of the country that had the previous revolution; in Italy, each city-state had its own bishop.[18]

Under such circumstances, a German prince came to rely on his state university as a way of getting hold of the clergy who studied there and thereby achieving some coordination for the territory. Luther was a professor of theology at Wittenberg, which had been founded in 1502 and which was the apple of his elector's eye. Hence, the elector supported Luther against the pope because the future of his own administration was involved. German professors played a prominent part in the Reformation from then on, notably in formulating the Augsburg Confession, the basis of the Protestant League. Even the Diet of Worms, while condemning Luther, gave theological faculties the right of censorship. The Diet itself took the revolutionary step of calling on nonpapal German theologians to examine the pope's case against Luther.[19]

The period of revolutionary upheaval had a double beginning. Revolution first broke out when Luther nailed his Ninety-five Theses to the church door in 1517, attacking the papal hierarchy as mediators between laymen and God. Then the princes themselves became reformers in 1525. They fought the peasants and Anabaptists who would have installed an individual religion in every village. They then struggled against the emperor, "protesting" his decrees against the Reformation. Open war broke out in 1546, and the Protestant League was at first crushed; but by allying itself with France the League defeated the emperor in 1552. The Peace of Religion in 1555 empowered the princes to reform their respective territories.[20]

There followed a period of arrogance on the part of both "Parties of Religion," Catholic as well as Protestant princes. Then came their humiliation in the Thirty Years' War, 1618–48, fought primarily between the emperor and France or Sweden, the protecting powers of the Protestants.[21] A century later came the golden age of Germany, 1763–95 or –1806, a time of great poets and thinkers, including Goethe, Schiller, Fichte, and Lessing.[22] Finally, World War I led to the abolition of the princely dynasties, paving the way for Hitler, a pre-Reformation type who became "pope, bishop, monk, and council in one person."[23]

The Reformation shaped German character and institutions in ways that lasted for centuries. It accounts for the German disposition to "protest" with violent criticism rather than compromise, for the harshness of the police, paternalism, the combination of independent lofty thinkers and obedient civil servants, for German efficiency, bookishness, and passion for systematic thinking.[24] The states of the Reformation were the first to separate civil from military affairs and to create civil administration and civil service for matters formerly handled by the Church.[25] Until the unification of Germany in 1866, the large number of German states competing with each other for the services of professors and civil administrators promoted both high quality of personnel and a unique kind of freedom; one could move elsewhere if one had a conflict of conscience with a given regime.[26]

England came next in the series of world revolutions, because it was the most backward country in relation to the Reformation. In Germany, a Protestant prince became head of the Church in his own state, but there were many princes and they were held in check by having to belong to a Party of Religion as well as by the theological faculties of their universities. In England, such was not the case. Henry VIII became a kind of king-pope when he became head of the Anglican Church. In 1535, he created the point of pressure leading to eventual revolution when he beheaded his Catholic chancellor, Sir Thomas More, "keeper of the King's conscience."[27]

It is a peculiarity of English history that only the Glorious Revolution of 1688 was called a revolution and that the preceding phases of the actual revolution were called the Great Rebellion and the Restoration. They really formed one continuous period from 1640 to 1691, in which the English gentry established the power of the House of Commons over church and state. It would be more appropriate to call the three phases Puritan Restoration, King's Restoration, and Anglican Restoration. The Puritans claimed to restore the liberties of Englishmen, and Charles II stole the term for the Declaration of Breda as a word of reconciliation—for he in fact recognized half of the Puritan Restoration. William of Orange in turn promised to restore rights and liberties.[28]

The English Revolution was of course really a great innovation, not a restoration. It was the technique of the Puritans to appeal to old traditions, precedents, common law, Magna Carta in order to advance their cause. There were important ingredients of canon law in what were formerly the common laws of England and the pope loomed in the background of Magna Carta. The Puritans' "common law" was an invention of the seventeenth century.[29]

Cromwell gave England a new vision of her future and a vigorous start toward it. The vision was of England's mastery of the seas and an imperial commonwealth, a Western World, beyond them. The start was the building of a "New Model" of the navy, and the Navigation Act of 1651 gave a tremendous boost to the growth of British shipping by requiring that all goods sent to or from British ports be carried in British ships.[30]

The period of revolutionary upheaval, 1640–91, was not immediately followed by a period of pride. That came several decades later and lasted until 1774, reaching its climax in 1763 when the English "had enough arrogance to tread the Colonies, France, Ireland and the plantations all under foot at once."[31] There followed a period of humiliation, which lasted until 1815, comprising the Napoleonic wars as well as the loss of the American colonies. Later came the golden age, 1846–1900.[32]

The dominant English national character shaped by this revolution was that of a gentleman, a relaxed but passionate fighter, disciplined by his ritualism of daily life, such as dressing for dinner; independent as a landed proprietor, with a penchant for understatement; unsystematic, shunning introspective reasoning, preferring to muddle through with instinctive presence of mind as a guide to action, with a religious faith in the future and his country's role, typified by Cromwell's famous statement, "Never is a man lifted higher than when he does not know where he goes."[33]

English insularity has tended to treat the English Revolution as a family affair. But it is important to emphasize that it was part of the European series and had universal significance. It "saved Portugal, the Netherlands, Belgium, and many other small nations in Europe from annihilation," "raised scores of political movements all over the world," and "set up the English Parliament as the Mother of Parliaments."[34]

The next world revolution was the French, because France was the most backward European country in relation to the English Revolution. The latter was conducted by the gentry and eventually established the sovereignty of Parliament. In France, the king had absolute power and the Estates General never even met between 1614 and 1789. In England, the gentry lived on their estates and had functions of local leadership and responsibility. In France, after the *Fronde* (an English infection in which nobles sought to limit the king's power), the king kept all the nobility, including the gentry, at Versailles, thus depriving them of their grass roots base.[35]

When the king moved to Versailles, he also created a fatal tension with Paris, which had been the capital and indeed much more. In the Middle Ages, the University of Paris was "the brain of the Occident, the School of all Christendom," on a par with emperor and papacy. This medieval role faded with the Reformation, but Paris as the biggest city in Europe was a major concentration of the city-dwellers, "bourgeoisie," the future carriers of the French Revolution. Paris was strengthened in this role by many Huguenots, by this time largely bourgeois, who settled there, where the law expelling them from France was not enforced. Thus, the two pressure points leading to the revolution were the slighting of Paris and the revocation of the Edict of Nantes, banishing the Huguenots in 1685. The upshot was: "at Versailles a privileged class without functions; in Paris a functioning society without privileges."[36]

The ideas that channeled these pressures as they exploded in revolution were of course those of the Enlightenment, notably of Voltaire and Rousseau: deism, liberty, equality, the natural rights of the individual, humanitarianism, the appeal to reason against tradition. These ideas were spread during the eighteenth century by the lodges of Freemasonry, which became the political organization of the European reading public. "It was the expression of the desire of contractors, artists, scientists, to build a new world."[37]

Using reason to dissolve traditional bonds isolated men as individuals, but their liberty to act on their own implied opportunity to act, which had to be based on private property, whether in real estate, money, or talent. Capitalism thus became an inherent feature of the French Revolution, but it worked better in France than in other countries to which it was exported because it was balanced by more complete equality of citizenship.[38]

The revolution broke out with the storming of the Bastille in 1789. The period of volcanic eruption lasted until 1815. It acted first internally, then externally, through the revolutionary wars. Napoleon conducted most of the latter as a true child of the revolution, spreading its seeds over Europe, but he was finished when he flirted with becoming a legitimate and hereditary ruler.[39]

Then came the Bourbon restoration, a period of incubation which nevertheless upheld the results of the revolution, followed by the July Revolution of 1830 as a kind of epilogue to the great upheaval, leading in turn to the period of arrogance, in which the bourgeoisie went in for orgies of capitalism and corruption, led by a bourgeois king who said, "Get rich!" There followed the abortive Revolution of 1848, which initiated the period of humiliation: two worker insurrections, then real Caesarism under Napoleon III, whose unsuccessful wars culminated in defeat by Prussia in 1870. Not until 1875 was the Third Republic fully established.[40]

Unlike the English, the French Revolution went in for written constitutions—fifteen of them by 1875—to organize a country three times as large as Britain, since aristocracy and traditions were swept away and reason was to be the guide. But the written constitutions were backed by an unwritten one, which included the sovereign role of Paris and her salons as the center of political, intellectual, and artistic life, as well as the cult of the French language and the role of the écrivains as a permanent source of inspiration.[41]

The doctrine of universally human natural rights logically led to the emancipation of the Jews, and Napoleon granted them equal rights as citizens of France. France was thus the first European society to realize a completely secular state. The emancipation was put to its decisive test in the Dreyfus affair and, thanks to Zola and other *écrivains*, it stood the test. "The non-Christian side of French Jacobinism is really its most Christian side. It offers to the Jew a common meeting-ground on the basis of humanity." Adam became the symbol of a unity that preceded the division of Jews and Gentiles. After emancipation, "the Jews became the natural bodyguard of liberalism all over Europe."[42]

The nation-state, with its messianic nationalism outbidding Jewish messianism, was a child of the French Revolution. In the Middle Ages, nations were geographical sections of Church councils, but the *natio gallica,* reminiscent of Roman Gaul with its natural boundaries, was the only one that corresponded to a single secular king or prince. Through the French Revolution, France, with Paris as its capital, its single language, and its largely natural boundaries, came to be looked upon as the model on which all nation-states should be patterned. This eventually led to the Balkanization of Europe.[43]

The ideas of the French Revolution nevertheless brought unification to Italy and to Germany, lay behind the Civil War in the United States and the emancipation of the serfs in Russia, and brought about the universal franchise in England and Germany. The metric system was established in France and spread out from there, as did the vogue of expositions and of fashions in ladies' dress. The craving for sensational novelties, including newspapers, was the counterpart of French rationalism, because reason, rejecting the *ancien régime* with its traditions, depends on another kind of revelation—the new. This spirit accounts for the belief in progress and the invention of the technique of invention in the nineteenth century. It further explains the cerebral quality of French eroticism, the special role of women in French civilization, the one-generational character of life, and the destruction of family ties in the modern world.[44]

The last of the European revolutions in the second millennium was the Russian.[45] Russia was obviously the most backward country in Europe in relation to the French Revolution and hence the place for the next one to break out. Its huge area, hostile climate, vast illiteracy, and poor communications made it extremely difficult to organize in the way that France was organized around Paris. There were few cities and hence few bourgeois. The Russian Orthodox Church had never sought to change the world as the Catholic Church had. The government depended mainly on exports, notably of timber and grain, for its financing. There was little industry, and such modernization as there was came from Western capital and capitalists, by whom Russia was exploited like a colonial area.[46]

One point of pressure for the Russian Revolution was the martyrdom of the Decembrists in 1825. It marked the final estrangement between the government and the youth of the leading classes, who had absorbed the ideas of 1789 from France. A second pressure point came with emancipation of the serfs in 1861, which was partly the result of French ideas about human liberty but was incomplete because it gave the peasants liberty without property and hence left them resentful and land-hungry.[47]

After 1825, the youths who went abroad to study became the Russian intelligentsia out of which grew the Bolshevik party, which planned and executed the revolution and which has governed the Soviet Union ever since. Their sufferings gave them the right to govern. They seized on Marxism because it gave them something to say, a new language with which they hoped to dominate the rest of Europe as revolutionaries, even though they realized that Russia had almost no proletariat to carry out the revolution. They themselves were not proletarians but came from aristocratic or well-to-do backgrounds—Lenin and Trotsky, for example. The criterion for admission to the party was not proletarian descent but "revolutionary disposition."[48]

The Russian Revolution was the first in the European series that was consciously planned. Lenin and others studied the French Revolution, particularly the Commune of 1871, to learn applicable lessons. Such consciousness led to prematurity. There were revolutionaries long before there was a revolution. So, whereas the French Revolution had an epilogue in 1830, the Russian had a prologue in the abortive revolution of 1905. Lenin, however, recognized its prematurity and stayed clear of it.[49]

The revolution proper broke out in November 1917, when the Bolsheviks seized power after a brief attempt at a bourgeois-type revolution under Kerensky failed. But its true birthday was the signing of the peace treaty of Brest-Litovsk soon thereafter, thanks to Lenin. That took Russia out of the war with Germany and enabled the Bolsheviks to replace patriotism with economics, confronting the task of thoroughly organizing the Soviet economy from within. Russia was a colony of western capitalism no longer.[50]

It is to be expected that the Russian Revolution would have a rhythm as did the preceding revolutions, but no such rhythm can be calculated in advance. Thus far it is possible to recognize a period of restoration and reaction beginning under Stalin in the mid-1930s following the initial upheaval. He restored czarism minus its alliance with western capitalism. This period ended with the downgrading of Stalin under Khrushchev, who began the period of arrogance.[51]

But the Russian Revolution is only part of what has been happening in this century. The two World Wars reached beyond Europe and constituted the World War revolution, of which the Russian is the eastern wing. The Bolsheviks, including Stalin, aimed at an eventual worldwide communist revolution and so did not recognize the World Wars as the real world revolution that they were. Even the Russian Revolution was made possible by three exhausting years of war beginning in 1914, which mobilized the peasants and proved that the czarist regime was not competent to organize the country.[52]

Unlike the Russian Revolution, the World Wars were unplanned. They took Europe by surprise and marked the end of European hegemony and of the dominance of the French-style nation-state. They led to an interplay of continents, pointing toward a planetary human society, a global economy, within which nations have only functional roles. If one includes in this revolutionary epoch the Russo-Japanese War of 1905 as prelude and the Korean War of the 1950s in which America confronted China, one can say that the world became round (that is, no longer Eurocentric) in Korea. By the time of Khrushchev the world revolution had burned itself out. Even if there is another great war, it will not be World War III, because the World War revolution has completed its structure.[53]

Looking at the series of total revolutions, other than the World War revolution, in the second millennium, one can discern several general features:

1. As noted in this chapter, each revolution breaks out in the most backward country and each follows a similar rhythm: point of pressure, upheaval, arrogance, and humiliation.[54]

2. Each revolution breaks out when the context of the pressure

point has shifted to its opposite. For example, Innocent III began the second half of the Papal Revolution when the emperor sought to unite southern Italy with his empire.[55]

3. As in France during the summer of 1789 and for Luther before the peasant wars, so generally there is a *grande peur*, a fearful sense that the old order has given up the ghost.[56]

4. Revolution often breaks out against good rather than bad rulers—e.g. Louis XVI rather than Louis XV—because the effects of bad regimes have lingered, overcoming the influence of good rulers who may follow them. That is, in a bad system, even a good ruler must be overthrown.[57]

5. Each revolution seeks a different kind of freedom, *from* something old and *for* the creation of a new order—even Lenin did, despite his "liberty is a bourgeois prejudice." There is a dialectic of revolutions whereby the oppressed in one stage are liberated in the next.[58]

6. Each revolution exports its forms to other countries most effectively during its period of humiliation, not during the initial upheaval—the French, for example, under Napoleon III rather than under Napoleon I.[59]

7. The leaders of each revolution after the first are akin to the leftists of the preceding revolution, as Luther to the spirituals like Savonarola and Cromwell to the Calvinists. Conversely, the mother country of one revolution is largely immune to the next one but adapts to it superficially (e.g. France to the Russian Revolution), while the countries of older revolutions are more vulnerable.[60]

8. Revolutions begin without reference to space, with a program for all mankind, but then take root in a particular country and shape the national character of that country. Hence, no country can have more than one complete revolution.[61]

9. "Every national character arose because types of men existed that called urgently for a supplement or an antagonist." The revolutions emphasize one after another phase in the conscious human life cycle: the Papacy, old age; Italy, motherhood; the Reformation, paternalism; England, manhood; France, womanhood; and Russia, the rebellious adolescent son.[62]

10. Revolutions create institutions that go on, like nurseries, producing a particular national character, and are thus in a sense immortal. But after several centuries of one-sided repetition, the

type becomes impoverished, a caricature of its former self, and it needs enrichment by others. The forms of a new revolution regenerate the stagnant older ones and today all are learning from each other.[63]

11. Among the most significant of these institutions are the holidays that are inserted into the calendar to symbolize the respective revolutions—e.g. Corpus Christi, the German princes' birthdays, Guy Fawkes Day, Bastille Day, May 1, and November 7. They educate succeeding generations in the traditions of the revolutions.[64]

12. After a revolution divides the old and the new, a third force, one of reconciliation, later embeds the revolution in the Christian era as a whole: the Cistercians (Bernard of Clairvaux) after the investiture controversy, the humanists after the Guelphic struggle, the Jesuits after the Reformation, Methodists and other pietists after the English Revolution, the romantic school after the Jacobins, still incognito after the Bolsheviks.[65]

13. Each revolution adopts a new political language and the series of languages forms a dialogue. For example, Germany praised paternal methods because Italy had praised maternal. The interdependence yet spontaneity of these utterances shows the unity of mankind, as one spirit makes its way through the whole series.[66]

14. Each revolution has its own eschatology and leaves the preceding one behind: the pope leaves behind the emperor's Last Judgment by becoming himself the judge of the world, but his fall is foretold as the coming of the Antichrist; Luther says that the pope *is* the Antichrist and awaits the coming of the Kingdom of God; the Puritans work *in* the Kingdom of God but fear self-conscious enlightenment, the fall of Milton's Lucifer; the French deify the Luciferian individual genius but envisage the fall of humanity into decadence and bestiality; the Russians leave the bestial orgies of capitalism behind but postpone the classless society in which history is to end.[67]

With the Russian and World War revolutions, the series of total revolutions comes to an end and so does the second millennium. It has been a unique process of becoming one world, by which all humankind has come to live in simultaneous communication together on one planet, in short, "world" history in a special sense.[68] Notwithstanding the worldly spatial obsessions of these revolutions and their consequent attacks on the Christian era, none has abolished it. The Church is still there, it is older than the second millennium though tainted by it, and it supplied the fearless souls who made world history. Becoming one world is in fact a phase of the advance of the singular against the plural, which is the essence of the Christian era.[69]

CHAPTER 16

INTRODUCTION TO
THE THIRD MILLENNIUM:
PLANETARY HUMAN

WE NOW STAND at the close of the second millennium of the Christian era and on the eve of what may become the third. It is not certain that there will be a third. If we do not end the second and its "world history" soon, another world war may mean the end of all human history. History is not predictable, but we can discern questions posed by the second millennium that the third will need to answer if it comes, and rhythms begun by the first two millennia that the third can be expected to round out into a complete whole.[1]

In the Christian era's advance of the singular against the plural, the first millennium saw the triumph of one God over the many false gods; the second unified the earth and the whole world of nature but "we have yet to establish Man, the great singular of humanity, in one household, over the plurality of races, classes and age groups .... They pose the questions that the third millennium will have to answer." The preceding chapter landed us on this doorstep, showing how the World War revolution directs us toward a planetary human society.[2]

The main question facing the third millennium is how to win

power over human times. The second millennium enabled men to master space but at the cost of losing their time sense, time rhythms, and power to shape time. Technology has enabled men to cover more and more space in less and less time, fragmenting time into smaller and smaller bits. Above all, the ties between human generations have been broken. Industrialization has pervaded all aspects of life. There is no preindustrial life left to draw on. Modern society is governed by "the Law of Technology: every advance of technology extends space, shortens time, and breaks up the group with which we worked hitherto." Human beings in the postindustrial age must attain the fullness of *all* the times (*die Vollzahl der Zeiten*) together, which were revealed serially in previous history.[3]

Women are by nature time-oriented, linked to past and future; brides give birth to children and mothers transmit family traditions. So we are now coming to *woman's first political hour*. The second millennium is ending in nihilism because men have lost their time sense; but women are to redeem them through renewed solidarity of love and faith, again and again. Nihilism will become only a stage that recurs in the ceaseless renewal of society and the continued creation of humanity out of nothing. On the other hand, women should acquire the secret of the space axis of the Cross of Reality that is natural to men as wooers and possessors; thus women can complete their Cross of Reality. In this way, both men and women are to become complete human beings. This is an example of the unification of humankind in the third millennium.[4]

There will also be a need to revive some aspects of tribal life, because of the modern deterioration of speech and family (both of which were created by the tribes), and also because tribes evade spatial ties (as nomads do) and value bonds between generations. The tribal revival should not only be selective—excluding human sacrifice and the warpath, for example—but should also be related to the development of the planetary socioeconomy (*Gesellschaft*) for which it is needed as an antidote, to balance coldness with warmth and intimacy, uniformity with originality. Ideally, such an economy would make people so interdependent that war would become impossible; but tribalism can be dangerous. Fascism and Nazism were premature rebirths of tribalism in this respect.[5]

What is badly needed—and not premature—is the widespread formation of small personalized teams of people who would work together for periods of five to fifteen years—for example, teams in factories or even groups living in small towns or in the countryside. These groups would make components of a manufacturing process, and would supervise themselves. They would develop group pride, team spirit, originality, and zest in their work, unlike the atmosphere in huge factories today; and their commitment to stay together for a predetermined period would help them develop a sense of time that is now unknown to workers paid by the hour and living from one payday to the next.[6] "Since the successive stages of an individual's biography and the shifting demands of industrialized society both involve us in a repeated change of roles, the breath of life must be allowed to take hold of us again and again with original renewing power, lest whole drab stretches of life and of mankind remain uninspired."[7]

An experiment in combating "the coldness and barrenness of human relations in the Machine Age" was begun with the work service camps in Silesia (1926–32) and Camp William James in Vermont (1939–42). These camps brought together young people from different backgrounds and classes of society—college students, farmers, and factory workers, who volunteered to spend several weeks to a year of their lives living together and working for the needs of the rural community. Working, thinking, and playing together was the basis for genuine communication between these widely differing social strata and for integration of bodies, minds, and souls. They also came in contact with an older generation, which matured the young and rejuvenated the old. The Silesian camps were conducted before unemployment was a problem, but with the Great Depression they bore fruit as a means of integrating the unemployed with the rest of society and conserving their labor power by keeping them active. The camps turned the unemployed from a liability into an asset, thus helping to generate a new social order. Camp William James was used as an example in the planning of the Civilian Conservation Corps; later, the Peace Corps drew inspiration from it. Service camps for youth all over the earth, a "planetary service" or "peace service," would help to unite humanity across national differences. Such service must be voluntary, not compulsory, in

order to give people a holiday or "Sunday" experience of renewed inspiration in an age when the machine makes them
forget how to have holidays. Such service, with its total devotion,
is also an example of William James's "moral equivalent of war,"
which will be increasingly necessary as the unified world socioeconomy makes war impossible.[8]

The socioeconomy is increasingly planetary but it will not be
one economic "system." Each of the total revolutions of the second millennium tended to produce a different economic order,
and capitalism and communism are only the last two. They are
now moving toward each other, the Soviet economy seeking
ways of decentralizing while in the West giant agglomerations
are becoming more public than private, regardless of ownership.
But both still suffer from the way modern industry alienates the
time of human lives, as mentioned above. The economy of the future will be pluralistic, polyphonic, a mixture of forms rather
than any one pure form, for life involves a shifting balance of
contradictory forces. To yield to any single trend means death.[9]

Territorial states and their rivalry with the Church were the
central themes of the space-minded second millennium, but in
the third, the state will recede in importance. The totalitarian
states of this century are mistaken efforts to cope with problems
of the third millennium using means created for the second.
States are now being subordinated to the global socioeconomy,
which reaches across territorial boundaries with airplanes and
earth satellites, for example, and the future of states depends on
how they fit in. We are entering a planetary age in which religions, races, and countries live in a single, common time-space
and borrow traits from each other: Islam, India, China, Eastern
and Western churches.[10]

Thus the Church will confront its daughter, the world economy, rather than the world of states, and it will need new forms
to accomplish its perpetual function, setting a model of Christian
living, in a time when industry has alienated people from each
other. Instead of education of children, emphasized since Luther
and the Jesuits, adult education should be emphasized, and instead of the Lutheran parsonage, small groups of people from
contrasting backgrounds should represent Christianity incognito
without ecclesiastical authority or denominational labels. They
should begin by listening to their members curse the troubles of

living in today's industrialized socioeconomy. Thus the preaching Church should become a listening Church, hearing confessions of social rather than individual sin and then achieving a loving and understanding response, setting experience in better perspective. Such should be the Johannine Christianity of the future, acting as a good Samaritan to the tired souls of a workaday world, inviting people to meet together in hope without requiring faith, awaiting inspiration by the Holy Spirit, the healing spirit, which comes when two or more are gathered together. As people commune together in this way, they might shed the armor of class, party, profession, or race that separates them and thus move toward the unification of humankind, which is the goal of the third millennium.[11]

The third millennium thus wrestles with the third article of the Creed, whose theme is the Holy Spirit. "The revivification of all dead branches of the single human race, the reinspiration of all mechanized parts of the single human life, is its double concern."[12]

CHAPTER 17

CONTRASTING VIEWS

ROSENSTOCK-HUESSY'S COMMENTS on other thinkers place his own thought in reciprocal perspective.

MARX

Karl Marx, following Hegel, used dialectical logic as his method and hence missed insights that the grammatical method brings. Marx thought in terms of "I" and "it," mind and matter, subject and object. There is no place for "you" in his system and hence no place for the actual life of Karl Marx, who was a "you" called to analyze capitalist economics and to defend the disinherited proletariat. Thus there would be no place for men like Marx in his classless society. Therefore, the classless society will never exist.[1]

Marx's dialectical materialism professes to make men masters of history, but mere knowledge does not yield power over human affairs as it does over nature. Marxism with its universal formula "tries to put mankind into the straitjacket of natural science," but when "a man is not invited to give his consent by a spontaneous 'yes' he is obliged to say 'no' lest he cease to be a man." Claiming to know men completely leads them to do the opposite; the proletariat that was to abolish the state established a superstate. Neither Marx nor the Russian Bolsheviks were proletarians. In theory, Marxist dialectic sets a "speechless antithesis" against a "speechless thesis." In practice, Marx and his followers abjured the thesis (bourgeoisie) out of love for the antithesis (proletariat), which was really their thesis in the first place.[2]

Marx was also wrong about capitalist exploitation being the cause of proletarian suffering, depriving labor of the values it creates in order to increase profits. It is not a matter of higher wages or profit sharing. "The irresponsibility of the employer for the *reproduction* of the forces he hires, uses, and eventually destroys or wastes is the curse of capitalism." The capitalist was "freed from all responsibility for the political, moral, and educational order of his country." Hired by the hour like electricity or other natural forces, the proletarian is divorced from his own longer time rhythms and is "deprived of the power to weave past or future into his own day of work." He is subjected to a concept of time as mechanical recurrence, the kind that occurs only in the dead world of physical nature.[3]

Interpreting all history as a series of class struggles and revolutions misses the "dialectic of millennia" with its duels between tribe and empire, empire and Israel, Israel and the Church. Even with regard to the second millennium A.D. Marx interprets all revolutions by projecting his theory of the communist world revolution backward into earlier revolutions that were quite different, and he misses the coexistence and interplay of revolutions made possible by the Christian era. "Marx's vision of the individual being molded into a kind of type by the specific organization of his society is true," but he did not see the rich variety of human types other revolutions created; capitalists and proletarians were not the only revolutionary classes. Marx's principle of totality as applied to revolutions is immensely fruitful, however, as opposed to mere national histories that miss the wider relationships. But neither he nor Lenin expected that a communist revolution would break out first in Russia, the most backward country. "The revolution of our time consists of two quite unideological World Wars, and the brain revolution of Marxism is only a partial reflection of these wars into an anti-Czar group called

Bolsheviks." But Marx did consider the world revolution a nonideological event. In that he was right.[4]

NIETZSCHE

With Nietzsche, as with Marx, there is no place in his own system for him as a "you," a man who was called to act. He was a victim of his time, with its superstition that everything could be reduced to "I." He eventually went mad in his solitude because of this superstition. He was right in believing that God was dead in that time. The philosopher's "I" is atheistic. People in Nietzsche's day worshiped "the individual" or "the state," mere idols. In speaking through the mask of Zarathustra, Nietzsche was really on a pilgrimage toward the Living God and in fact few did as much as he to revive God in men's hearts. Such was the effect of his role as Antichrist. Nietzsche (and Marx as well) borrowed his greatest secret from Christianity; he renounced personal success in order that his action might live all the more strongly. Nietzsche misunderstood the Christian dualism between worldliness and otherworldliness, interpreting it as nihilistic, "yet he gave a secular version of the real Christian otherworldliness in his vision of supermanliness and the self-overcoming of life."[5]

FREUD

Like Marx and Nietzsche, Freud lacked the insights of the grammatical method. Instead of you-I-we-it, he created an ersatz Cross of Reality: I-reality-superego-id. As "the last individualist," he began with the "I," analyzing the individual from that point of view only. There was no place in his theory for himself as "you." But in practice, his life followed the normal Cross of Reality, beginning with being called "you," going on to "I will undertake it," the "we" of the psychoanalytic movement, and finally the "he" whom we can study objectively.[6]

DARWIN

Darwin in turn lacked the grammatical method, inasmuch as he based his principle of natural selection on animal life before the origin of man and hence of language. The human race goes in for inspired selection by word of mouth, not natural selection. A soul gripped by an earthshaking event will bear fruit "only if its bearer undergoes his conjugation as 'you,' 'me,' 'we,' and 'they' (or 'it')." "The struggle for existence is a struggle within the social body of language and fails as often as it succeeds." It is really a struggle for recognition, for which life is often risked.[7]

Darwin saw struggle in the *outer* world, not inside society. He saw that outer world as chaos, not order and unity. Mere detached observation of facts always makes the world appear as a jungle. But that is only a fraction of the whole truth. Darwin's "survival of the fittest" misses the role of weakness in human as distinct from animal life. It is the source of plasticity, "the only way of conquering the future."[8]

Darwin, Marx, Freud, and Nietzsche freed us from space-thinking, time-estranging idealist philosophy. They were "dysangelists," prophets of bad news, the suicide of Europe that came with the World War revolution. Our point in time is thus marked by our living after them.[9]

SPENGLER

Deeply influenced by Nietzsche, Spengler was another atheist who wrote during the time when God was dead. His *Decline of the West* was conceived in 1910 and thus represented a pre–World War I point of view, though his first volume was published in 1917. He expected the final downfall of the West in two or three centuries, but it actually occurred in the World Wars. They were the suicide of Europe to which Spengler contributed by his resolve to die proudly with the West.[10]

Spengler wrote only an onlooker's "they" history, not a "we" history of shared memories based on speaking together. He also sinned against the grammatical method by excluding names, holding them to be only "sound and smoke." Names-using language would connect cultures into one history.[11]

Spengler was a pagan and hence went in for cyclic thinking. He ignored the true roles of the Jews and the Christian Church because they transcend his culture cycles. He was right in regarding the second millennium A.D. as a distinctive epoch in history, as does Rosenstock-Huessy in his books on European revolutions; but Spengler separated it completely from the first millennium, filling the latter with the cycle of the "Arabian" culture and the former with the cycle of the "Faustian" culture and allowing no bridge across, no Christian era of which they were a part. The paradox of Spengler's system, which he acknowledged in conversation with Rosenstock-Huessy, is that although his six cultures were like separate boxes, he, inside one, could know what was inside the others. It is the Christian era that gives all times access to each other, thus making possible the unity of history. In effect, Spengler wrote on the basis of the Christian spirit that he denied.[12]

The downfall of the West has occurred, but its ideas and values gave the whole world, not just the "mother landscape" of Europe, a common pattern, which is now disintegrating too. Our only salvation is to become planetary humans, to "resurrect into new times and new spaces beyond the grave of our hopes." Spengler is to be contradicted because "there is a freedom that here and now can upset all historical laws through death and resurrection."[13]

T H R E E

FIRES OF
INSPIRATION

CHAPTER 18

SELECTED APHORISMS

MANY OF ROSENSTOCK-HUESSY'S more striking sayings could not readily be woven into chapters. Some are presented here as aphorisms, though they were not written as such but had to be extracted from the texts in which they were embedded. For the sake of smooth reading, editorial elisions are not indicated. Quotation marks are not used since all items are quotations. Sources are shown in parentheses at the right. For symbols used, see pages 117–120.

The only way to surmount an inspiration that has become inadequate is to anneal it anew in the fire of a better inspiration.

(SI 574)

Whoever speaks blazes up. Whoever blazes up speaks.   (V 324)

In one who speaks the surge of the spirit must always hold sway. Only another, be it himself at a later stage, can clarify what bursts out of him.   (U 35)

We ourselves never ignite the light of reason; it is kindled in us.

(V 459)

Under the impetus of conversation we become new creatures of our creator. The author of the Platonic dialogues remains their author. A genuine converser becomes the creature of his conversation.   (SII 408f.)

"Everything is relative" is the sentence with which thinkers devalue our existence. But for you or me as speakers every absolute is more incomplete and impoverished than what is relativized.   (SI 49)

To speak means to participate in the evolutionary adventure of speaking humanity.   (SR 63)

Whoever speaks believes in the unity of mankind. And he believes that the unity of mankind is not produced by physical or political or economic or racial reasons but by our faith in speech. We all believe in the Holy Ghost, the Oneness above and around our particular way of looking at the world. The individual's greatest freedom has as its corollary the spirit's greatest necessity. If all men are bound by one truth, then my-truth makes sense. If it does not, I go mad with my freedom.   (SR 184)

By language men are able to act as One Man. Thus we create peace, fellowship, security, continuity. By speech we take possession of the earth together and march into the future as One.
                                                                                    (SI 23)

The religion of a man rests on the names that induce him to act jointly with others. These names may pass away, but in their day they are mightier, more valid, and contribute more to history than private relations to a pretty face or to blood kin.   (SI 569)

The numbers of space withdraw names in order to unify space. But names carry out the unity of time by settling on us out of belief in the unity of all times. Finding time means creating life. Unifying spaces means abolishing life.   (SI 199)

We live out of the future into the past and this life force, this calling, grants us our name.   (SI 76)

To be called by his true name is part of any listener's process of becoming his true self. This is part of the process of being fully born. The United States of America did not exist before they were called the United States of America. Cartesian blindness to this reality of names disfigures most investigations by psychologists, sociologists, and historians, who do not know that they are paralyzed by their Cartesian origins.   (I 66)

Language, because it is life, is subject to the law of life, that it originates from death; life means overcoming death. When we live we must change every moment in order to keep alive, we must breathe. When we breathe together we speak, we are inspired. It is thus a struggle of the common life against decay through death.   (G 119)

Mankind covers the whole of space and the whole of time more and more, because language conquers more and more space and time, and the reunification of languages unifies this universe of ours perpetually. Language creates one unique being through the ages.   (LaLo 11)

In living language all particular sentences, songs, speeches, books, national languages, literatures are only detached tones of a monotheistic but polyphonic symphony. Our sentences have meaning only in the polyglot of the choruses of human history.
                    (Si 369)

Things are predictable because they do not speak. He who speaks is unpredictable.   (V 656)

Their leading character should be restored to vocatives and imperatives. That would do more toward the elimination of atheism and cynicism than all pious tracts together.   (AG 89)

If my word holds, although only I have said it, because I believe that I have said it: he who speaks so believes in God. Only he who gives no credence to his own sentences is godless.   (V 628)

The devil is the speaker who does not stand behind and is not overtaken by his word.   (V 567)

The godless denies God's presence, not the words of religion. Then it becomes senseless to say it is high time. Thus if present is without elevation over past and future, no God lives to punish and avenge. Then a blind fate rules the world, and our consciousness becomes a curse and a mockery on our slavery.   (V 125)

Fate means what we are at the mercy of. And we are at the mercy of what cannot yet become word.   (V 380)

Only the word makes what has happened into history.   (U 188)

The law of language says: what is most central or primary in an event is articulated last.   (SII 839f.)

The tragedy of Greek philosophy was, and is to be found in modern times again, in misunderstanding the process of hearing and learning. The process of thinking in the schools of philosophy is a tradition of dialectical contradiction between teacher generation and student generation. The students stored the words of the master in their memory. Then their own living experience came into play and asked for articulation. And it could find articulation not in supplementation to the teacher's doctrine, but only in diametrical opposition. The new experience was articulated abruptly.   (SR 139f.)

The power of recognition that enables us to identify our own new experience with the record of past experience is a power that transcends logic and definitions. The power of identifying us with people who express their ideas in other terms requires a quality of the mind that is much rarer. It requires the superior power cultivated by the Church and in the family: the power of translating eternal truth into the language of the times for the sake of mission and education. The power of translating fuses the different ways of understanding.   (SR 140)

Two thousand years ago, an utterly new phase of speech was entered upon. Never since has any speaking group of the human race based its existence on the fact of one individual language. A new principle was proclaimed: all languages may be translated into each other. Practically speaking, all languages rest today on the common basis of translations of the Bible. Just the same, seceders may build hard and fast walls between each other, and these prison walls of language occur time and again whether between nations or between professions.   (SR 161)

Language may die and does die, and kills the spirit of its speakers eventually. It is the essence of language to be momentary, fluid, fleeting. Hence a word has its full truth only among the people between whom it spouts, and at the moment at which this happens. This explains the authority of the words of Jesus. Truth cannot be tin-canned and sent around in boxes. Schools cannot teach the very best, because they usually are so far away from the best moment for saying the best. Language becomes rigid, classic, formal, abstract, hieratic. In a petrified language, which claims authority although it doesn't gush forth as in the author, we taste the decay and impotency of the reality which they tried to express.   (SR 162f.)

Powerful language must be unrepeatable yet audible to us ourselves. The speeches of statesmen that are distributed in advance to the press mostly do not need to be delivered at all. A prayer that is written in advance is to a degree more unreal. Our Lord hears everything the first time. Then the word wrests itself modestly out of the heart and surprises its speaker precisely as its hearers. Here the cautious action of language is revealed. It had to guarantee that we heard ourselves yet did not become shameless as with mere repetition.   (AG 69f.)

Without speech man would have no time, but merely be immersed in time. Animals are time's toys. Men conquered time when they began to speak.   (I 115)

The present, whether it be an hour or a whole era, is not a natural fact but a constant social achievement. True presence of mind, the power to live in the fullness of time, has to be won arduously and preserved by perpetual vigilance. When a man rises above his future, which is the imminence of his death, and beyond his past, which is the reminiscence of his origins, he enters the present.
                    (I 94)

Only since people mocked and guillotined priests and nobles have they given themselves to the illusion that speaking costs none of life's time. When the journalist became the commanding general of society and stock exchange rates his communiqués, every important difference between the instantaneous thought of the joker, and the legislator giving laws for descendants, and the sacrament holding good for all times, seemed abolished.   (SI 95f.)

The abundance of time is not quite the same thing as the fullness of time. Most people who have plenty of time never fill it to the full. They throw it away. To gain time, and to learn how to regain time, is the content of mankind's story of earth. It is the easiest thing in the world to work all the time, compared to the incredible difficulty of spending one hour or one day of rest in a proper way.   (O 14)

Mercury's and Vulcan's work fever surrendered Germany to the Ludendorffs and Hitlers. The compulsion to be industrious leaves no leisure for political perception.   (SI 45)

For the solitary and for peoples, time has the majestic character of a womb, frightening, overwhelming, because the perpetually changing rhythms spring from it, which vibrate between high time and everyday life and which we must help to victory on pain of our own downfall.   (V 53)

A great new event is more than an additional paragraph to be inserted in the next edition of a book. It rewrites history, it changes the past because it initiates a new future. Anyone who looks back on his own life knows how completely a new love, a new home, a new conviction, changes the aspect of his past.
                                                                    (O 5f.)

He who honors his past has future. And every man should claim only as much past as he has future.   (V 57)

The gift of prophecy is the power to embrace a total experience at the beginning.   (J 88)

Terror does not exist for the space thinker. Whoever has nothing to decide can contemplate without terror the victims of syphilis or of world wars. No new time begins without profound fright.

(U 312)

The war historian recognizes that God enters the times whenever people commit their lives for re-tying the connection between beginning and end of history.

(V 109)

Nobody can see history happen. The already-happened part of the Church is visible, but the part living and happening today *must* happen through suffering and martyrdoms. Else the Church is dead.

(V 42)

First-rate experiences are not gained through the eye. The not yet visible must keep a step ahead of the visible; else nothing first-rate happens. Teilhard de Chardin realized that nobody could have known the first "Roman." The common sense of all times struggles against this law of delayed visibility. Paul, Saint-Simon, Paracelsus remained invisible to their contemporaries, and in the third millennium all continuation of life will depend on whether there will still be voluntary incognito.

(V 33f.)

Life can never be painted. One must hear and scent it.   (UM 144)

Seeing puts us in an outer space, even facing our neighbor. But hearing I share the common inner space of all voices.

(V 58)

Visible life is chilled and diminished life. The highest life, the engendering, conceiving, inspired, devoted, in short all creative life needs the times of night and day, darkness and brightness in succession.

(V 43)

God is invisible. Hence the human who wants to be His image must be invisible too. All who educate for a visible ideal are pre-Christian.

(SI 144)

God can never communicate something to me as long as I think of myself as an I. God recognizes me only as a you.   (SI 105)

The Living God cannot be met on the level of natural reason

because by definition He crosses our path in the midst of life, long after we have tried to think the world into a system.   (C 96)

Salvation always comes from where nobody expects it, from the depraved, from the impossible. It can only become salvation in that no human cunning can fathom it, in that it does not evolve within creation but freely enters creation as the Divine.   (HK 285)

God is incalculable. He makes some children and some adults very good indeed and others very wicked. He is quite indifferent to the date at which we were born. It is equally difficult at all times to live the good life.   (I 70)

One who keeps faith with the God in his heart seeks Him not in the rainstorm, fire, earthquake, but in the still voice.   (SI 42)

The concept simulates God's absence; but since God is present, He can only bless us to the extent that we give up fancying ourselves opposite Him. All we can experience of God plays duet, trio, quartet because our heart plays a part.   (SII 69f.)

Atheism befits the expert, the chemist, and Mr. Darwin, who conceived the struggle for existence. But atheism would only be pathetic for someone who gratefully trusts in his highest inspiration. There he trusts in God.   (D 105)

Man's judgment is always capable of revision. But Creation cannot be revised: it speaks a final language. God does not speak to us in words, He speaks in forms and creatures. For the discussion of the values of a plant, an animal, or a civilization, our logical yes and no are of little use.   (O 191)

God's mind is just as much a metaphor as His elbow. Our mind is not nearer to God than our body.   (SII 228)

A beloved name always points beyond my acquaintance. He who does not love defines. A defined god is my prisoner; he is a thing, for Aristotle the prime mover.   (V 329)

Everyone knows of God whose soul out of love has had to call somebody by the right name and been permitted to recognize him in virtue of this act of love.   (V 329)

We experience the world by our work. We experience God without work. We experience Him in will-lessness; we experience Him in suffering. We experience Him in the progenitive act of love, and the first form of our potency, our generative power, is not sensuality but the word wooing for love.   (H 80)

A nation never forgets its interval in the open, between fear and faith, hate and love; for in it this section of humanity came into contact with God.   (O 474)

The man who believes in nothing still needs a girl who believes in him.   (V 744)

"The good works" of yesterday are never "the good works" of tomorrow. Every faith gives birth to *its* good works. Hence if a faithful human goes to work, the old guardians of the law do not acknowledge his good works as works of faith, but only see that he does not do the works they have already declared to be good and pious.   (V 42)

The Greek experience of time as original newness is *right*. The only trouble is that it is transient. The soul, in distinction from the mind, cares for one time only, God's Time, Eternity. But the trouble is that the soul never knows this unless it is lacerated by the manyness of mentalities, by a conflict of more than one time.
                                                                        (CE xviii)

We find in the victory over tragic conflict the deepest meaning of our destiny.   (C 202)

The power of a holiday consists in the ascendancy over tragedy. Any time must tackle its central conflict, bring it into some rhythm, and finally ennoble it by a holiday. As long as the greatest conflict of a period is not faced, all its minor conflicts will reopen, under its pressure. We have left peacetime thinking and wartime action completely unreconciled. Thinker and warrior

have no common history. If we could create it, the community
spirit would be reborn.   (C 214f.)

Education, inspiration, the good life, express themselves in rhyth-
mical order. Rhythm is the mutual begetting of opposites:
weeping and joy, winter and summer, victory and defeat, birth
and death, make up the rhythm, if and when we tackle them as
opposite numbers and do not leave them to accident. The fires
which warm the hearts of men light up rhythmically; if not, they
destroy us.   (C 208)

The religious, the poetic, the social, and the scientific consciousness all must have their grammatical representation in our souls.
We must ever again be unwritten pages, but become You at the
call of a command before we can be "I"s, "We"s, and "It"s. The
death of the soul immediately follows the extinction of the last
appeal to the power of a man to accept his call.   (SII 578)

Body and mind, It and I, are grammatical figures of the soul, the
You. You are able to polarize yourself in It and I, body and mind.
But woe to you if you imagine you have a body and you have a
mind. Your kidney is as mental as your head.   (SII 274)

Without modesty there is no growth of the soul. If the soul were
an It or an I, thing or god, it would not need modesty. But a
human soul, as You, conceals itself.   (SI 778f.)

Modesty is the veil under which life can change. With the veil of
modesty the time necessary for change is won.   (V 366f.)

Psychoanalysis concerns itself now with the destruction, now
with the overcoming, of modesty. Hence its contradictory, am-
biguous character. The soul cannot be healed by simply opening
itself and thereby surrendering its peculiar tension.   (SI 779)

The soul needs an incognito against its associated consciousness;
it must not know who it really is. What we know of ourselves is
what is dead in us.   ([b] 258)

To myself there is only the detour via prayer, for the simple reason that nobody can know himself. We children of earth must crouch masked behind a thousand social skins. The soul can walk unmasked only in the presence of its Lord God. (S1 68f.)

He who can only show that he has attained his self-assigned purposes has failed in life. How could a purpose set by me comprise my self, me who have produced this purpose as a tiny tip of my self? (V 615)

Plato's ideas are abstract gods. Philosophy is reduced and therefore neutralized truth from Parmenides to Hegel. Only the whole of language together is true. But the Greeks began to say: "Being" and "I am that I am" (which is not in the Bible, but in its Greek translation), and there the academic world of ideals began. "I am" together with "I was not" is meaningful. But "I am that I am" is idiocy. (V 506)

In Plato's city, Socrates would be the first to be executed by the guardians. (S1 498)

Wherever people swear by the word of a master and wherever a master conjures, gods are invoked. Marx invoked the god of the proletariat. (U 10)

He who cannot attribute Hölderlin's insanity to Hölderlin lacks a relationship to Hölderlin. One who does not lose his mind over certain things has none to lose. (U 326)

It is the error of enlighteners to think that they can make do with one "ideology." Real life is nourished by two speech sources. One language calls inspired people to their functions; the other—from below upward—makes this function subsequently understandable to the five senses. (V 443)

No political association can rest on a single ideology. Only the reconciliation of conflicting ideologies constitutes the life of a political association. (G 182)

The biography of a real human being includes a deeper secret than the fulfillment of one ideal or one philosophical system.

Ripeness is everything. To take every step in life at the proper time is man's great personal mission.   (MM 68)

Absolute Idealism, absolute Materialism, any -ism does not take into account the paradox that every man must have more than one philosophy, during his life, and that a man's soul must be bigger than his mentality. All philosophies are partially true. Reality must be realized by more than one approach. The human soul is challenged today to see the relativity of all philosophical systems; hence, to survive any one of them.   ([SoLa] 22)

Philosophies have their time. It is a misunderstanding to attribute perennial character to any particular philosophy. Philosophy is the expression of a zeitgeist. Philosophies must be buried at the right time. The Jesuits know that Thomism is dead.   (SI 619)

It is not the goal of man to become a philosopher, rather the goal of a philosopher must be to remain a real man despite his thinking. Man is the measure of all his parts, even of his head.
                                                                                     (U 232)

Body and soul are not objective parts of the outside world. They are the two constituent elements of two different worlds which we ourselves are constantly building by our own actions and reactions. The world of bodies embodies our way of *working* and the world of souls our way of *living*. There is a third world which we are building all the time by our way of *thinking*. Our mind is a creator too.   (O 86)

The mind is a member of the creaturely world. Its objects outside in reality remain free from its disjunctions. *The world has no rational structure.* But [the mind] itself is the way from chaos to order.   (IR 82)

Most "Christians" unsuspectingly go along with deriving the higher from the lower, the living from the dead. Today nobody laughs at this unthinkable thought. It is supposed to be scientific.
                                                                                     (UM 144)

Negations never add a new quality to propositions, and dialectic as a method of thinking is prone to empty statements.   ([z] 7-047)

In an experiment science repeats its readings several times. It follows that science lets only what is repeatable affect its statements. All unique processes are basically unsuitable for scientific observation. Hence much is true that is unscientific.

(SII 231, 234)

Every man is a temporal being. Tomorrow, when I perhaps might know how to help him, it is too late. No natural science method can ever guide men, because it lives by experiment, and every experiment limps behind events for the duration of the experiment itself and its evaluation.   (V 727f.)

Poetry is not irrational at all. It is much more rational than mathematics. The lyrical mood descends into the dark depths of our body and carries the light of reason into the bottomless pit of the fires of sex, fear, jealousy, ambition, greed, and pride, which are born in these depths.   (OR 58)

Every value in human history is first set on high by one single event which lends its name and gives meaning to later events. We have seen many movements called "crusades," but they derive their name, if it is properly given, from the First Crusade. Crucifixion and resurrection would not be known as everyday occurrences in our lives if they had not happened once for all, with terrific majesty.   (C 103f.)

Evil increases automatically. Inertia, laziness, cowardice, death are self-multiplying. Good "is" not, except by propagation; it is not in any man, but originates only between. No man is good. But the word or act that links men may be good. And by link-work evil has to be constantly combated.   (I 26f.)

The moralist and the creator live in different tenses. If we mix the ethical with the political aspect of life, we shall never be able to do justice to our own best actions. True action is not responsible to so-called ethics. A vital issue rises above the known good and evil because it leads into the unknown. The results of all our crucial actions are hidden from us. Many precalculated actions do succeed. But they all happen in a field from which the full inbreak of free and divine future has been excluded by careful organization. Here life is immured in the categories of past and present.   (O 720f.)

The supernatural should not be thought of as a magical force somehow competing with electricity or gravitation in the world of space, but as the power to transcend the past by stepping into an open future. Nature is not free to rise above her entropy and inertia. But man is more than nature because he can go against his nature. His heart can arrest social habits and physical causes as they impinge upon human life; it can make the future grow by taking the first step into it.   (C 123)

"Nature" is the world minus speech. It is a misleading word, because voices call us into life first of all, and water, earth, and wind may concern us only after membership in society and participation in language secure us roped fast above the abyss of nature.   (SI 43f.)

We call nature just one attitude of ours in which we forbid ourselves and the things of the background to have intercourse with each other. The background is the realm of objects. Anything put in the background ceases to have the right to talk to us, or to be talked to. To use the word "nature" is not the statement of a fact but the execution of a death warrant. In the world that is flooded with natural science, we ourselves are left exanimate on the battlefield.   (LuPh 16)

Any natural scientific method, as far as it is applied, neutralizes the geologist or physicist or biochemist, obliterates their personal, social, and political experiences. Hence, the sciences develop a habit that is disastrous for the social thinker. The terror of revolution, war, anarchy, decadence, must have made an indelible impression before we can study them. The scientists who sit in objective judgment before they are overwhelmed simply disable themselves for their real task, which is to digest the event.   (I 17)

Academic prejudices may be summed up as "obsession with

space"—especially with external space and its corresponding ideal of "objectivity"—to the utter neglect of time. Our division into departments represents the result of centennial space supremacy. Our college methods are all methods developed for space. This is really disastrous in the humanities and social studies because man is a peculiarly temporal being. It would treat all realities as things external to the mind, things in which we as thinkers have no roots, and which may accordingly be manipulated without reference to the common destiny in which we and they are jointly bound. This may do for physics. It will not do for human society.   (I 92f.)

We get at no man with common denominators and collective labels. Every book about alliances, associations, classes, nations, churches that works with denominators achieves the opposite at best. For it stimulates us to do the opposite of that which the denominator predicts about us. Sociology is thus presumably not a science? It can become one only if it does not exert that stimulus of labels. For us sociology is the science of the ways and processes of actual and therefore only partially knowable men. One who was wholly known would have ceased to be active; he would hence have become unactual.   (U 17, 19)

Watchmen are not to be watched. The Russians attempt it. But they will have no luck with it. For those who watch the watchmen become sleepy too. This sleep follows upon the fatigue toxins of the world process; repetition lulls to sleep. Thus being unfatigued is the condition for the persistence of a social order.
(V 683)

Most people think today that all organizations of size, states, corporations, labor unions, are rational, legal, and mechanical. However, the only group which is really exciting at any minute and full of surprises because it is fully alive also is perfectly unsystematic, irrational, antilogical, and the poorest organization on earth. I mean, of course, the family.   (C 138)

No youthful nation including America has ever settled vital questions by discussion. Against class hatred, sacrifices alone can help, sacrifices of a completely irrational character, which cannot be discussed beforehand but must impress themselves by their symbolical potency. Our faith in forces greater than man's intelligence, a charity greater than any social intelligence ever warrants, and unbending hope in the victory over the worst fiend animate those who by their personal decisions and sacrifices enable us to cooperate and to live inside of some semblance of order.

(C 52f.)

In welding more than one local group together, the energy called authority is indispensable, the power that allows people in different ways of life to turn to one and the same source of inspiration. Authority secures the *cooperation of people who differ.*   ([gy] 4)

External war is the father of domestic law. The community of war times is always the new community. Peace writes down the constitution which was tested in war.   (O 671)

In the peculiar case of America we find a Freudian repression which forbids all mention of the interplay between war and revolution. The four turning-points of American policy were each preceded, at a distance of half a generation, by a war. The experience of war sank deep into the womb of the time, and fertilized the common understanding of a change to come. When this new phase of life appeared, the fact that it had been begotten in the preceding war was overlooked.   (O 665)

The loss that threatens through the vanishing of war is loss of the ability to distinguish play and seriousness. War is the main case of deadly seriousness. Every act in which I am ready to commit my life comes close to war. How is one to endure in a world in which nothing more is absolutely serious and in which consequently nothing new can be born? Must today's boundaries all freeze, if only wars loosen boundaries? The abolition of war would only be possible through the creation of a process that alters boundaries.   (D 16, 18, 21)

In secular psychology which begins with the child, we are told that it should pull itself up by its own bootstraps and become itself, express itself, live by itself. The tone of the spirit reverberates first within us when we obey. The child which is not made to obey is denied the power ever to command.   (I 73)

Our whole society has forgotten the means of regeneration which enables both the individual to survive the stages of life and his society to survive succeeding generations. The secret of eldership lies in the fact that an old man is through with his own life but not at all through with life. He watches all the later generations with a loving wisdom which alone can reconcile their strife. He is the great pacifier, the guardian of life's continuity, because people know that he alone is free from personal or partisan aims. Therefore he is peculiarly the regenerative force in society. It is the expectation of one day becoming elders that should carry us through the full cycle of our own lives. The production of elders must take precedence over all social activities. Without elders, who embody the secret of survival, the group itself is lost.   (I 104)

One reason why we have forgotten the role of eldership is that we have come to take the succession of generations in the history of mankind for granted, whereas it is really a perpetual achievement. The natural relationship between the generations is deadly warfare, which constantly threatens to put an end to history in any significant sense. The supreme function of education is to be the strategy of peace which links the generations into the history of the race. But this does not mean the abolition of all conflict. Only by facing the conflict between the generations can we overcome it.   (EdSt 7f.)

No social science can communicate any truth to a student or reader who has no experience of peace, and for that reason, of the evil conquered by peace.   (SR 31)

We humans come to ourselves always too late. Our foresight never sights our self, but always one lying out beyond ourselves. What the young beauty experienced the ugly old matron can know of course, but this experience can say nothing more to her beautiful young self.   (U 213)

The young depend on the choices made for them by their elders. An heir is not somebody who can choose what he shall inherit.

He does, however, determine the background of the next generation.   (C 221)

Shaped life attracts younger, more shapeless life. The young always try to inherit everything which there is to inherit from the
past.   (C 221)

We are emerging from a period in which parents abdicated in
favor of their children. They became satisfied with being their
children's best friends. The slogan of friendship has overshad-
owed the problem of peace between different generations who
pass through their experiences at different times, and yet must
make these experiences with full vigor. It has made the old
childish, and the young skeptical.   ([gy] 18f.)

A father's mind should enter into the impulses of his son. Father-
hood is rethinking the world in the light of one's children. Why is
God so inexhaustibly original? Because he rethinks the world for
every generation of his children.   (C 231)

The Fioretti of St. Francis are very often quoted today. But "fioretti" is no sentimental metaphor. Francis knew very well the
ruinous results of a situation in which the past encroaches upon
the future. Each day must be freed and lived like a new present,
unknown, unheard-of, incalculable, virgin territory.   (MM 21)

One-half of the world is regular and recurrent, lawful nature, and
the other half is love, change, grace, surprise. We could not take a
railroad train to go and propose to our sweetheart without this
dualism.   (O 189)

The creation of the world is not at all complete. At every moment
originating life and developed life exist side by side. The revolutionary and sacrificial life, devoted to change, coexists with the
hard and fast recurrence of old forms.   (O 191)

The application of chemical or physical concepts to society loses
all meaning in the face of man's power for the "re"-making of life.
By the modest "re" man is separated from the rest of his fellow
creatures. The riddles of our human existence lie in the fact that

we are reproducing a changeable kind. That is why we are neither angels nor bees.   (O 735)

Old forms of life can stay alive only as long as new ones unburden them from the stagnation that comes with repetition.

(C 120)

Innovation is a condition of our aging, just as repetition is a condition of our staying young. The proportion between the inheritance of acquired characters and the acquisition of inheritable characters is our riddle.   (V 20)

The law of deterioration from inspiration to routine holds for speech as for other phases of life. Every time we speak we either renew or cheapen the words we use. Hence Christian language can be abused like any other. Yet when the bread of life has gone stale, it has been refreshed again and again by a new transubstantiation. These transformations of living speech-in-action are the real sacrament of the Spirit, and if we walk humbly under our bankruptcy today, we may hope to hear the Word spoken once more.   (C 130)

The future does not stay open automatically; it has to be re-opened by your own inward death and renewal. Not steady movement in one direction but continual redirection, breaking through old ruts, is the formula for progress. All routine, all secondary forms of life decay when they are not keyed up again by the bursting of one new blossom, by one step into the unknown and improbable.   (C 83)

Modern man is daily fortified in his inoffensive, pragmatic Confucius style of living. To this man, the future always comes as a complete surprise. The war was a shock. Bolshevism was a shock. This modern man strikes me as the queerest combination of the best-informed and the most surprised human being. The facts they call knowledge deal with living. But "living" is but one-half of life, the repetitive and predictable part. The other half is the creative agony of dying and being born.   (C 57)

The sufferings of the incognito, the share of every man in the still quite incomprehensible future, must be paid in advance. The entry of genuine novelty requires suffering. All peoples and ages have credited bearers of spiritual authority with such an initiative into the future with the single exception of the last eighty years. Hence the past century has produced ever fewer credible men. The authority not to speak like the scribes but like one who has power is exactly measured by the strength of soul with which one renounces becoming approved right away.   (H 142f.)

How else should a new inspiration come to us men, if we did not offer ourselves as a vehicle for this inspiration? Man must be torn open again and again by the plowshare of suffering.   (SII 872)

Science since Darwin has abandoned unity; John Dewey abandoned suffering as our basis of understanding the world. For the reason of unity we had made all our history since Christ one common enterprise for all men who were converted to this Oneness. And for the reason of revelation through suffering, we had built up a hierarchy of values: according to the degree a man had suffered, we listened to what he had to reveal.   (C 56)

Man's life, social as well as individual, is lived at a crossroads between four "fronts": backward, forward, inward, and outward. It is obviously fatal to fail on any front. Yet it is equally obvious that no individual can move adequately in all four directions at once. Therefore life is a perpetual decision. Both mental and social health depend on preserving a delicate mobile balance. Integration, living a complete and full life, is accordingly not some smooth "adjustment" we can hope to achieve once for all, as popular psychology imagines: it is rather a constant achievement in the teeth of forces which tear us apart on the Cross of Reality.
                                                                                              (C 168f.)

Man shall start new fellowship incessantly. We are less ourselves when we remain within our own shell than when we incorporate our neighbor. In fact, man without this growing fellowship becomes a split personality. Inner unity within myself is only achieved by outer unity with others.   (FY 24)

One who lacks the will to monogamy can never know what true

love between the sexes should ripen to. One who is not prepared to suffer for the truth can never know what the truth is. One who does not defend his fatherland will never understand what freedom is.   (SII 888)

If Job had not suffered, and if Ruth, the young Moabite, had not married Boaz the Jew, Christ could not have appeared in the flesh. The presufferings of the pious are their blessing on an evil, on death, on danger, expressed and thereby acknowledged as God's ways and therefore blessed! The secret of the prehistory of Christianity is presuffering.   (SII 436f.)

Nothing great in this world can be achieved without great expectation. The expectancy of the listeners is a condition for every communication. Only in response to the messianic expectancy of all peoples could the Messiah come. And only what fulfills a longing finds an enduring place in history.   (AG 17f.)

In society we must respond, and by our mode of response we bear witness that we know what no other creature knows: the secret of death and life. Any glorious work bears the stamp of eternity if it was called into existence by this sign in which Creator and creature are at one. *Respondeo etsi mutabor* ("I respond although I shall be changed"); a vital word alters life's course and life outruns the already present death.   (I 14f.)

No pagan logic admits the "although." The Christian era has added this step into novelty and continued creation. Newness is not man-made. That we may become changed men, *although* we have to suffer, even to die, is incomprehensible to a Greek mind and yet it is the everyday experience of any living soul. In the *respondeo*, although I may be changed, the scientific mentality is transcended. Creativity comes to self-forgetfulness. He who remains inside his own consciousness is incapable of experiencing real newness.   (I 66f.)

This is the criterion of what is human that has been laid down by Christianity: how a man can be eternal in the moment, how he can act *once for all*.   (A 108)

Through its creation of future, Christianity has endowed man, in-
dividually and collectively, with the power of having a life history. In the cyclic, pagan view of history everything we do has
happened before; nothing of permanent value is achieved. Man
gives his acts an eternal, i.e. "once-for-ever," meaning by throw-
ing his whole personality on the side of life that should now
come forward, at each moment. But he can select what should
come forward only because one end of time draws his heart at
each step into the future. The uniqueness of the present derives
from the uniqueness of the end. Hence only if history is one can
our present-day acts have a once-for-ever meaning. Unity is not
given, not a natural fact, but a common task of some ninety-nine
generations to date.   (C 71f.)

The Dogma of the Incarnation is our sole guarantee against lapse
into polytheism, which is widespread today. Human values are
many, and philosophy reflects their pluralism unless it has a universal standard for the perfect man. One Man must rightly be
called God for all time, or paganism will return again and again
as often as inspiration lifts men out of the daily groove of the law.
Jesus showed his divinity by taking on himself not earthly glory
but earthly suffering. Thus, instead of exploiting the hero worship of the masses, he emancipated them by sharing his divinity
with them. But one condition was attached, the Christian condition that henceforth no individual could become a god on his
own account. The communion with God became one for all men,
and in every generation the same coincidence of God and man
that started in Jesus is realized by those who keep together in
One Spirit. That is the meaning of the Church as the Body of
Christ.   (C 107f.)

The rhythm that interrupts four other rhythms must keep itself
free from these already existing rhythms. Thus the first law of the
Incarnation was: its rhythm was inaudible and all the more invisible. The content of the four gospels consists primarily in the report of this fact, that nobody, including the apostles, perceived
this new rhythm.   (V 264)

Jesus' death on the cross came at the last moment that still gave
the apostles time to live through a second generation in the new

rhythm before the destruction of the Temple. History can never be made by one generation. Christ's Passion likewise came at the first moment at which it had become senseless to convey his own Son's power to the true Israel. Herod's government annulled all of Israel's promises. The flight to Egypt hence was like the exodus from Egypt under Moses written in reverse.   (V 271)

Jesus remained under the Jewish law to the end of his first thirty years. It took him the time span of one generation to outgrow the synagogue. His obedience consisted in his patient walk through life. The risen Christ may walk with all men. He could not belong to the ages if he had gone at nineteen into the desert and founded a sect then and there. It is the whole content of Christianity that we are free, but that we arrive too late at our own freedom for fully wielding its liberating forces ourselves. Our own time is a station between the times which our freedom rejects and the times which our patience prepares.   (C 223)

Jesus proved that even death and absolute failure could be fertile. His Resurrection means that even the most valueless part of life can be turned into an asset not for the individual but for All Souls. Death became a carrier of life between souls. Herewith the last frontier of the soul was conquered, and its complete realm could begin to evolve.   (SoLa 23)

The story of Christianity, both in the lives of individual Christians and in the life of humanity, is a perpetual reenactment of the death and resurrection of its Founder. Only by his great outcry, "My God, my God, why hast thou forsaken me," did Jesus become our brother. All of us are bankrupt at times; by giving up the power of his spirit for this one moment he created his equality and unanimity with all men. Faith cannot live unless it remains intermittent; that bitter truth admits death where it belongs in our belief, as a bringer of new life.   (C 90)

Christianity is the founder and trustee of the future. Future means novelty, surprise; it means outgrowing past habits and attainments. At the center of the Christian creed is faith in death and resurrection. This alone is the power which enables us to die to our old habits and ideals, get out of our old ruts, leave our dead selves behind and take the first step into a genuine future.

(C 61f.)

Christianity always begins with a new form of Sunday when it rises from the dead. The yoking of future and past is the history of the Church, and the Christian week does this by placing Sunday, on which we anticipate the future Kingdom of God, ahead of weekdays which carry on the patterns of work inherited from the past. This is the sublime reason why Sunday is the first day of the week, instead of the last. In this way, the inspiration of Sunday slowly melts the frozen forms of weekday routine.   (C 204f.)

Anybody whose eyes have been opened to the fact that life depends on dying knows that the resurrection has its severe laws. A wounded heart does not recover in the spiritual world without a change in the visible world. Resurrection never does enthrone the spirit in the same place where it left one body, as though nothing had happened.   (C 145)

Anything a man is ready to die for is stronger than anything people merely live on.   (O 542)

Only one who dies for his way of life confers immortality on this way of life.   (Si 63)

Theologians have made a great pother about the early expectation, and subsequent delay, of the second coming. The debate is pointless. The combined expectation *and* delay of Christ's return is the contradiction on which the Christian lives, a tension which is the paradoxical essence of Christianity. By anticipating death we actually postpone it, and thereby generate a unique historical process which is the Christian story of salvation.   (C 71)

The conflict with pagans made early Christians vividly aware of what they stood for; but by 1850 there were not enough confessed pagans left to keep our hearts awake to the conflict.   (C 62)

If all people in the world called themselves Christians, the cause of Christ would be irrevocably lost. For as soon as the Christians were only among themselves, their sins would no longer be successfully uncovered.   (H 24)

The sin against the Holy Ghost cannot be forgiven because it is the only one for which there is no reparation. The Spirit is too free and too defenseless.   (AG 75)

I would be inclined to reverse Luther's axiom about the value of primitive Christianity, and would like to say that I could not believe in the Holy Ghost unless it changed its forms of expression mercilessly.   (SII 832)

The true meaning of the expression "Holy Ghost" is lost if we do not hold fast that it opens the spirits of different times to one another.   (SII 828)

The belief in universal inspiration, in a permanent guidance of the Saints and the Holy Ghost, is the outstanding difference between the historical adventure of Christianity and the natural religions. Inspiration is perpetually transforming humanity.
                                               (O 178)

The words preached and read in the suburb are uttered tentatively and in good spirits. By good spirits, we mean without giving offense to anybody. Important words always give offense. They make a difference. The Holy Spirit is not a "good spirit" but the better spirit!   (SI 226)

The processes of the Spirit have not been discerned very clearly since the Reformation. Perhaps the second article of the Creed, i.e. the sentences on the Savior, have monopolized the labors of theologians. The philosophers, on the other hand, have usurped the first article and, by isolating it, they have made it meaningless. But the third article of the Creed is the first article in our experience. The apostles experienced the Father through the Son in the Holy Spirit. In other words, before God came upon them as the spirit of Pentecost, neither the Son nor the Father was accessible to them. An experience of the Spirit will have to precede any understanding of the Son or the Father in the Trinity. The Church must fight the Greek arrogance by which our so-called minds are not considered the carrier of the One Spirit through the ages, but as the free agents of our little atomized selves. (I 71f.)

The Church is a teleological institution. It can be understood only in terms of its fruits, not of its causes. For a century or more, Church historians have practiced the method of reductionism. They have virtually explained Christianity away in terms of all sorts of sources, until nothing properly Christian was left. The effects contain the meaning, just as a newborn child has its meaning from tomorrow, not from yesterday. (C 162f.)

The reductionists debated the question whether the end sanctified the means. Every child knows that this is not the true question at all. Our ends never sanctify anything. The crucifixion is a scandal to any "healthy" instinct. If salvation had been Jesus' "end," this means would have been obscene. Jesus was sent into the world to do his Father's "end." (C 163)

Christ acquired a new faculty, the timing of the Spirit. He imparted to us this rightly timed spirit, this power not only to proclaim but also to obey these promptings in God's good time, neither too early nor too late. (I 70)

The West-East controversy with Lysenko about the acquisition of new characteristics is a question perversely put. Of course we incessantly acquire new characteristics and transmit them. That is the meaning of our history. Language transfers acquired characteristics. (SI 303)

People who have neither inherited something nor bequeathed something worth inheriting vanish without a trace. (E 513)

Marxism is an attempt to found a church on bread alone.
(MePp 17)

We today are sure that economic forces pull all the wires, but bread and butter is an everyday question. For that very reason it is not the permanent question of history, because history selects. History is the putting of different questions at different times.
(C 385)

In the long run the abolition of slavery paid in dollars. But long before, it had to be realized that slavery was untenable even if it paid. All economics are subservient. Nothing is anchored in the depth of history which is not first decided *regardless of cost.*

(C 213f.)

The basic law of all history: only where extreme resistance is overcome does a new origination become possible. Usually we live according to the law of least resistance.   (V 383)

We can drag too much history around with us, not only too little. The whole of history can be understood only when I know approximately the same amount about each time. What matters is the right relation of the parts to the whole.   (V 286)

It was an illusion that an empire ever reconciled between heaven and earth. But it was fruitful and indispensable. Fruitful error is the remarkable truth of all history.   (V 466)

The great revolutions succeeded because they achieved something that was necessary. True statesmanship and true direction of one's own life are guided by instinct for the necessary. Arbitrariness is the death of men and nations. The category of necessity is beyond abstract good and evil—a category of the true future.

(O 719)

Something can be just today that was neither right yesterday nor will be right tomorrow. All government becomes just only by being driven by an emergency.   (V 102)

Timely prerogative creates and restores actual government, legalizes conquest and force. The test of domination is success in this particular emergency. If it succeeds people will support or tolerate it in spite of its other faults. The secular state of the Reformation was the result of an emergency in religion and law.

(O 384f.)

The New Deal and the devaluation of the dollar are unthinkable without a preceding Bolshevik Revolution. The great revolutions

are eccentric, they exaggerate, they are brutal and cruel. But the
life of the rest of the world is regenerated by their outbreak.

(O 481)

It takes four or five generations to beget the perfect fruit. Types
like Pitt or Gladstone or Lincoln or Bach or Goethe had to be
ripened by a long succession of unbroken faith. Evolution is
based on revolution. Creation goes on as God's creation has always done. A thunderstorm of destruction clears the air; then
follows the low rustle of growth and reconstruction.   (O 466)

Our enemies almost always stamp us in their own image. In combating them we become like them. If we struggle against a police
state, it could be that we establish such a one.   (Si 468)

Every form of civilization is a wise equilibrium between firm
substructure and soaring liberty. Childlike people praise the liberty and ignore the substructure. They do not ask the price of
one's privileges. Pacifists, liberals, Protestants, Socialists, in their
genuine passion for improvement, forget the delicate equilibrium
that underlies a civilization. Mankind always stands on the edge
of barbarism and universal warfare.   (O 563)

Civilization, as a living body politic, is mortal. It is bound to die
by its own accomplishments. Death is the goal of life.   (O 563)

The anticipation of a Last Judgment looming over our own civilization is the best remedy against its inevitable downfall.   (O 561)

An event which has not settled something once for all is of no
importance to living men and women. A preposterous attempt, a
precursor, a stormy petrel becomes valuable when we bring it
into relation with the successful "once for all" achievement. The
"once for all" principle works like a great sieve, sifting out
quantities of superfluous traditions.   (O 75)

If we do not sense the one Spirit at work behind the spirit of different periods, we cannot be inspired by history. History is dead
so, and it is dangerous to play with the graves of the past. But
history lets us rise from the dead if we push behind the facts of

the day, and realize the sum of sacrifices and creative power hidden behind every little fact entrusted to us.   (SII 829)

Nothing in history can be repeated. If two events are to have the same effect on men at different times, the forms of the two events must differ.   (O 537)

The tree of everlasting life can grow only through successive generations of men reaching their hands to each other in one spirit across the ages. And *each generation has to act differently precisely in order to represent the same thing.* Only so can each become a full partner in the processes of Making Man; only so can life be as authentic in the last age as in the first.   (C 130)

Each generation differs. And neither race nor creed nor class has as much influence on history or politics as this mutual seclusion of one generation and all others.   (C 219)

The individual is not the carrier of history. Carriers of history are always three or four generations together. The centuries of the Enlightenment exalted Tom, Dick, and Harry to be independent choosers of their life history. Why can that never be? Because I with my ages of life am as deeply caught in the previous time and the subsequent time as in my so-called "own" time.   (V 76)

Men of the Enlightenment believed that they themselves could live without myth. They ascribed to every time a zeitgeist to which one abandoned oneself without restraint. But zeitgeist is only a polite word for myth. For every attempt to identify one part of the world, a single country, a single century, with the whole world and the whole of time, is mythical.   (F 9)

The Enlightenment condemned the West to fall when it entrusted ·
progress to the brain, the most backward organ.   (SI 20)

Public opinion is the form of the period 1789–1917 in virtue of which all speakers can be criticized. Wherever public opinion is manipulated, the period of this liberalism is spiritually extinguished. No man can become whole or rational who does not al-

ternate among being discussed, listening, and commanding, that
is, does not alternate between He, You, and I.   (SI 376f.)

The Communists cannot love, because for them no individual is
permitted to resist the world plan. Yet the Russian people can
love so strongly that they survive Stalinism.   (U 189)

The three temptations in the wilderness, today the official religion of the Bolsheviks, invited Jesus to have as comfortable a life
as other mortals.   (V 259)

The prematurity of their consciousness forced the Bolsheviks to
act "devilishly." The Bolsheviks have such rigid, dogmatic ideas
of the end that they do not take any particular political act today
quite seriously. All their own acts are opportunistic measures to
dupe the still "unripe" opposing forces. They will not keep faith
with anybody. Our situation is quite the reverse. We lack ideas
about the final goal. As the World War lacked war aims, so
"without ideas" we undergo the World Revolution. That is precisely our anti-Bolshevik role in it. Only so can we outweigh the
prematurity in the consciousness of the world revolutionaries.
Their ideology does not concern us. We have to retard and delay.
          (E 528f.)

Sharpening and preservation of antitheses—that alone is life in
the European sense. Much reason and much incalculability,
much order and much freedom, much ecclesiasticism and much
Christianity, much objectivity and much subjectivity, much so-
cialism and much individualism in clear and distinct development is the task of European culture. Much people and much
state is the contradiction with which our life preserves its fascina-
tion and its uniqueness.   (A 965)

Where is there place for the right relation of generations when
three generations of Russians have rebelled against their fathers?
This is the question of all questions for the world today. It is the
question for Europe, for the United States, for China, for Japan,
for India, how there can be hereditary forms in a disformed
world.   (E 514)

All natural-born forms have been washed away with the princes and monarchies. As ersatz, one has organizations, republics, and Soviets. But nature does not let herself be replaced by calculations. Where she has died only the Spirit which vivifies creates new forms. The Church guards the secret of these forms. Her own body is Spirit-worked form. She is a model for the peoples, of how they will have to let themselves be poured in Spirit-worked forms in order to continue.   (A 37)

It is unnecessary to deny this world: chaos denies itself. Modern man is crucified already. The salvation he needs is inspiration for his daily toil and leisure. For us the difference between worldliness and otherworldliness is that between finite forms already created by the past and the infinite breath of the spirit which blows in upon us from the open future. The other world is in this world as man's destiny, man's meaning.   (C 125)

The greatest temptation of our time is impatience, in its full original meaning: refusal to wait, undergo, suffer. We seem unwilling to pay the price of living with our fellows in creative and profound relationships. From marriage to teaching, from government to handicraft, man's relation to man has become noncommittal in the Machine Age. To be noncommittal means to keep all relations without important consequence, to rob them of their reproductive, fruit-bearing quality. Modern man's temptation to impatience accordingly expresses itself in the craving for panaceas and shortcuts. So men like Marx or Hitler or Huxley proclaim a "brave new world" that would put an end to history.
                (C 19f.)

The ancient world was cursed with dead spirits that could not die. Our mechanistic world is cursed with unborn inspirations that meet with no conception.   (SII 579)

There is a paradox about suburban man: he lives amid too much peace, but knows little peace within. He is a battleground for a hundred organizations and pressure groups. In consequence he plays safe. The prudence of the suburb begets a corresponding philosophy which pervades most popular psychology and sociology today: the philosophy of adjustment, of golden mediocrity. This doctrine means no real excitement, no real devotion, no real fight, no real love. The values and institutions on which we live were created by maximum effort. The philosophy of minimum life would never make possible one work of art, one discovery, one free constitution.   (C 14)

We can learn much from Lao-tse. In our urge for artistic creation we are in danger of not ripening the fruits of creativity because we strive for them too feverishly. Thousands of college people have forgotten the equally important problem of creative silence. We must cultivate the courage to stay silent for a while among the people with whom we live, so that when we do speak our voice will have become theirs.   (C 180)

We live in a strange society: the individuals are rather self-denying and civilized, often even weary of their power, but the groups composed of these anemic individuals lust shamelessly for power.   (I 100)

The world chokes our soul and plunges us into the original sin of society, the self-adoration of interests separated by the division of labor which the world requires.   (C 23)

In our own days, scientists begin to assume so much power that they are threatened by the same cancer that kills any powerful group or clergy, simply by imparting power.   (RI1 9)

Many a scientific mind hates to admit its polarity to the spirit of prayer. But hate blinds; and so science sees its nice academic world shaken by spellbinders. Practically, science called for Hitler because science no longer knows of its limitations. Scientists should crave their opposite: that white heat of speech during which men come to know God's will as differing from their own wishes and from any leader's will.   (JD 188)

Love and its liberty are too often confused with will, even by theologians. Love and will have as little to do with each other as a wedding ring with a cannon. Will is not free, for it must struggle for life; but love is free, because it can choose death.   (C 111)

All men kill, because they must seize something living in order to

live themselves. And all men die. The history of the human race
is accordingly written on a single theme: How does love become
stronger than death? The composition is recomposed in each generation by those whose love overcomes a murdering or dying. So
history becomes a great song, Augustine's *Carmen Humanum*. As
often as the lines rhyme, love has once again become stronger
than death. This rhyming, this connecting is men's function on
earth. But that this is our function we have only known since the
birth of Christ.   (V 759)

To be sure we must conquer death. Only that does not happen
through Darwinist survival, but solely through speaking across
death. Death is not overcome by not dying, but by our loving
beyond death.   (J 98)

EPILOGUE

ROSENSTOCK-HUESSY does not claim to have the last word. His thought is fluid, ever in process, and leaves loose ends along the way. Thus his great value lies less in what he inculcates than in what he stimulates. His many facets of unfinished originality inspire originality in us.

His interpretation of Christianity seems to me more appealing and more convincing than any other I have read. He is not an innovating heretic. He roots his views in the Bible, the Creed, and the continuing story of salvation in the Christian era. Yet he is not a narrow fundamentalist. Neither is he one of those liberals who water down Christianity to suit current moods in science or social reform. But he does call for new modes of life and worship in the Christian future. Thus he takes the Holy Ghost with intense seriousness; its inspiration goes on creating the story of salvation.

The Living God is accordingly the ultimate source of all creation, all emergent novelty. The problem of evil as defined by theologians does not seem to exist for Him. His creativity is inscrutable, it makes some people wicked, but it also leads to resurrection beyond death. In this sense, evil is overcome and in the process God suffers and dies too. Jesus' crucifixion and Resurrection in the life of the Church was thus the final revelation of God. In all life, suffering, the experience of an emergency (*Not*), is required for creation. The problem is to let it become creative, to follow God's will rather than pursue our arbitrary ends, to do what is necessary (*not-wendig*) to meet the emergency.

Spinoza was called a God-intoxicated man. Rosenstock-Huessy is speech-intoxicated, which comes to the same thing because speech is God for him. In this he is surprisingly close to information theory, as expounded by Jeremy Campbell in *Grammatical Man*, which makes formative messages the source of all order, somewhat as Whitehead's God is the persuasive source of order.

Rosenstock-Huessy's philosophy is logocentric, and by beginning with language it escapes the egocentric predicament of much philosophy since Descartes, because language involves at least two people, a speaker and a listener. In this sense, his philosophy is sociocentric too. A logical consequence is his grammatical method, using language as the clue to society. The reader will have noticed how it pervades the treatment of other subjects in this volume. Its primary emphasis on names instead of nouns, vocatives instead of nominatives, imperatives instead of indicatives, is a revolutionary approach to language.

The Cross of Reality, the culmination of the grammatical method, requires careful application. "Cross" suggests something rigid, static, spatial, yet the Cross of Reality belongs to a body of thought that emphasizes time more than space, plastic, growing life rather than dead matter. The great innovation of the Cross of Reality consists in superposing the time axis of preject and traject on the traditional space axis of subject and object, yielding a four-dimensional epistemology unlike anything else in the history of thought.

Hence, one must constantly remind oneself that the Cross of Reality is not an entity but a method, an interplay of four ways of encountering reality. Its four arms are therefore better indicated by adjectives: prejective, subjective, trajective, objective, or even better by verbs or adverbs when available, than by nouns.

It is only fair to apply this fourfold method to Rosenstock-

Huessy's own thought. Many readers who already know and are devoted to his writings may feel repelled by the present volume because it uses primarily an objective approach, seeking to clarify and relate meanings, whereas they love to read him subjectively, rejoicing in the swirling jungle of metaphors, swimming in the ocean of his faith. Yet my approach remains legitimate as long as it does not claim to be the only valid one, and I have sought to balance it by many direct quotations (including all of part 3) that convey the passionate quality of his thought. The historical chapters of part 2 express his trajective approach as well, and chapter 16 on the third millennium is essentially prejective, not predictive, calling for us to accomplish great things in the centuries to come.

Rosenstock-Huessy is a positive and forward-looking thinker. While warning against many chances of catastrophe, he inspires us with faith, hope, and love to do the seemingly impossible. He is the best answer to Spengler that I know.

While acknowledging his kinship to Bergson as a time thinker opposed to space thinking, Rosenstock-Huessy develops time thinking further by describing the rhythmic nature of human time, how we create a present by overlapping past and future, and the problem of timing, of doing what is necessary at the right time, neither too early nor too late. He also relates Bergson's two kinds of time to each other as stations of the Cross of Reality rather than being content with a sheer dualism.

This leads to the central role of holism in Rosenstock-Huessy's thought. It is not formulated and analyzed as in abstract doctrine, but pervades all other themes. A rhythm is a temporal whole, an epoch of history for example, and God's time is whole. The story of salvation is the process of humanity becoming whole (heil). Healing is making whole. The Cross of Reality gives us access to the whole of reality, despite its contradictory fronts. The soul is a whole, entire process of living. In marriage, the spouses form a whole of which they are members. Holism is the clue to Rosenstock-Huessy's stand against reductionism in all fields, against explaining the whole by the parts, the present by the past, the higher by the lower.

Many years ago, a German humor magazine defined a professor as "a person who disagrees." Specialists in many fields on which Rosenstock-Huessy touches, such as Egyptology, are likely to disagree with various details of his views, but I believe that an imaginative Egyptologist will also find clues that lead in original directions. I hope that the present volume will give useful orientation for this purpose. More generally, the discussions of tribe, cosmic empire, Greece, and Israel should be taken as sources of novel insight rather than factual detail, as ideal types to which historical data may not correspond completely, yet which help us understand them and their relationships. I find the explanation of how Greece came to be Greece particularly illuminating.

Likewise with regard to the future, Rosenstock-Huessy has already proved himself a prophet not only in foreseeing the rise of someone like Hitler but particularly in analyzing the generation gap. His insights into its importance, its causes, and its cure are fundamental for our time.

I also believe that Rosenstock-Huessy's insights into the ills of the Machine Age and its spiritual exploitation of human beings, and his suggested remedies, are worth careful study by sociologists and economists. They are likely to disagree in many details, but his novel approach, e.g. looking for ways of turning unemployment into an asset, may lead to original solutions. His ideas about, and his pioneering in, voluntary work service have already borne fruit in the Peace Corps and may be helpful in other directions, domestic as well.

Rosenstock-Huessy's views on the Russian and World War revolutions lend useful perspectives for dealing with political as well as economic problems of our time. We are indeed entering a planetary age and the economy is increasingly worldwide. The role of American conservatism in balancing Soviet prematurity, if wisely conducted, can lead to the right timing of further developments in planetary society, neither too early nor too late. Calling us from beyond that goal is the comprehensive unification of humankind.

NOTES

ORIGINALLY NAMED Eugen Rosenstock, Rosenstock-Huessy hyphenated his name with his wife's when they married in 1914, but he did not use the hyphenated version for his publications until he emigrated to the United States.

The most complete bibliography of his writings, compiled by Lise van der Molen, begins on page 155 of this volume. A less complete one is in G below, also published in English (New York: Four Wells, 1959).

Symbols used in the notes refer to Rosenstock-Huessy's writings as follows:

Books and Pamphlets

	Das Alter der Kirche. With Joseph Wittig. 3 vols. Berlin: Lambert Schneider.
A	Vols. 1 and 2, 1927.
AIII	Vol. 3, 1928.
AG	*Der Atem des Geistes.* Frankfurt a.M.: Verlag der Frankfurter Hefte, 1951.
AH	*Arbeitsdienst-Heeresdienst.* Jena: Eugen Diederichs, 1932.
AP	*Abbau der Politischen Lüge.* Frankfurt a.M.: Carolus-Druckerei, 1924.
C	*The Christian Future.* New York: Harper Torchbooks, 1966.

CE   *The Christian Future.* London: S.C.M. Press, 1947.

D   *Dienst auf dem Planeten.* Stuttgart: W. Kohlhammer Verlag, 1965.

E   *Die Europäischen Revolutionen und der Charakter der Nationen.* Stuttgart: W. Kohlhammer Verlag, 1961.

EC   *Europa und die Christenheit.* Kempten-München: Jos. Köselsche Buchhandlung, 1919.

F   *Frankreich-Deutschland.* Berlin: Käthe Vogt Verlag, 1957.

FL   *The Fruit of Lips, or, Why Four Gospels?* Pittsburgh: The Pickwick Press, 1978.

G   *Das Geheimnis der Universität.* Stuttgart: W. Kohlhammer Verlag, 1958.

H   *Heilkraft und Wahrheit.* Stuttgart: Evangelisches Verlagswerk, 1952.

HK   *Die Hochzeit des Kriegs und der Revolution.* Würzburg: Patmos-Verlag, 1920.

I   *I Am an Impure Thinker.* Norwich, Vt.: Argo Books, 1970.

IN   *Die Interims des Rechts.* New York: Four Wells, 1964.

IR   *Vom Industrierecht.* Berlin: Verlag Hermann Sack, 1926.

IV   *Industrievolk.* Zweite Aufl., Frankfurt a.M.: Verlag der Carolus-Druckerei, 1924.

J   *Ja und Nein.* Heidelberg: Verlag Lambert Schneider, 1968.

JD   *Judaism Despite Christianity.* University, Ala.: University of Alabama Press, 1969.

K   *Im Kampf um die Erwachenenbildung.* With Werner Picht. Leipzig: Verlag Quelle & Meyer, 1926.

L   *Lebensarbeit in der Industrie.* Berlin: Verlag von Julius Springer, 1926.

MM   *The Multiformity of Man.* Norwich, Vt.: Argo Books, 1973.

O   *Out of Revolution.* New York: Four Wells, 1964.

OR   *The Origin of Speech.* Norwich, Vt.: Argo Books, 1981.

OS   *Ostfalens Rechtsliteratur unter Friedrich II.* Weimar: Hermann Böhlaus Nachfolger, 1912.

PR   *Politische Reden.* Berlin: Verlag Lambert Schneider, 1929.

RI   *Rosenstock-Huessy Papers.* Norwich, Vt.: Argo Books, 1981. Chapters indicated as RI1, RI2, etc., because paged separately. *Die Sprache des Menschengeschlechts.* 2 vols. Heidelberg: Verlag Lambert Schneider.

SI   Vol. 1, 1963.

SII   Vol. 2, 1964.

SR   *Speech and Reality.* Norwich, Vt.: Argo Books, 1970.

U   *Soziologie.* Vol. 1, *Die Uebermacht der Räume.* Stuttgart: W. Kohl-
         hammer Verlag, 1956.
UM   *Der Unbezahlbare Mensch.* Freiburg: Herder-Bücherei, 1964.
V   *Soziologie.* Vol. 2, *Die Vollzahl der Zeiten.* Stuttgart: W. Kohl-
         hammer Verlag, 1968.
W   *Zurück in das Wagnis der Sprache.* Berlin: Käthe Vogt Verlag,
         1957.
WA   *Werkstattausseidlung.* Berlin: Julius Springer, 1922.

Articles and Chapters

[ax]   "The Impoverishment of the Type." In *Britain and Germany,*
         edited by Gardiner and Rocholl. London: Williams & Norgate,
         1928.
[ay]   "Symbol und Sitte als Lebensmächte." *Die Erziehung* (1928–29).
[b]   "Protestantismus und Seelenführung." In *Protestantismus als
         Kritik und Gestaltung,* edited by Paul Tillich. Darmstadt: Otto
         Reichl Verlag, 1929.
[bb]   "Der Sozialismus als Antithese." *Zeitwende* (1929).
[bba]   "Vom Staat zum Stamm." *Der Kunstwart* (1929).
[bc]   "Die Kirche und die Völker." In *Credo Ecclesiam,* edited by Hans
         Ehrenberg. Gütersloh: C. von Bertelsmann, 1930.
[bm]   "Revolution als Politischer Begriff in der Neuzeit." In *Festgabe
         für Paul Heilborn.* Breslau: M. H. Marcus, 1931.
[bn]   "Einleitung" and "Arbeitslager und arbeitsdienst." In *Das
         Arbeitslager,* edited by Rosenstock and von Trotha. Jena: Eugen
         Diederichs, 1931.
[e]   "Judas Ischarioth und die Preussischen Konservativen," by
         Ludwig Stahl [pseud.]. *Hochland* (1931–32).
[ea]   "Student and University Service to the Community." In *I.S.S.
         Annals,* no. 3. Geneva: International Student Service, 1932.
[f]   "Arbeitslager." In *Handwörterbuch des Deutschen Volksbildungs-
         wesens,* edited by Becker, Narciss, and Mirbt. Breslau, 1933.
[g]   "The Predicament of History." *Journal of Philosophy* (1935).
[gi]   "What They Should Make Us Think" and "What We Should
         Make Them Do." In *Annual Conference of CCC Educational Advi-
         sors.* Hanover: Dartmouth College, 1940.
(gy)   "Youth and Authority." In *American Youth,* edited by Winslow
         and Davidson. Cambridge: Harvard University Press, 1940.
[h]   "Planetary Man." *New English Weekly* (May–June, 1946).

[k]   "Was Bedeutet die Stadt für das Christliche Leben?" *Zeitwende* (1949).

[n]   "The Homecoming of Society." In *Adult Education, UNESCO International Conference in Hamburg.* Hamburg, 1954.

[t]   "Das Volk Gottes in Vergangenheit, Gegenwart, Zukunft." In *Juden, Christen, Deutsche,* edited by Jürgen Schultz. Stuttgart: Kreuz-Verlag, 1961.

[te]   "Stalins Einebnung und die Chronologie der Weltkriegsrevolution." *Zürcher Woche,* 1 December 1961.

[v]   " 'Im Notfall' oder 'Dis Zeitlichkeit des Geistes.' " *Neue Sammlung* (1963).

[z]   Articles in *The American People's Encyclopedia,* cited by volume and page, e.g. [z] 1-22.

Unpublished Materials

BeAf   "Before and After Karl Marx, Prophecies Fulfilled and Unfulfilled." Lectures at Union Theological Seminary, 1954 (transcribed 1985).

Br   Letters and other handwritten items cited by number: Br1, Br2, etc.

EdSt   "Education, the Strategy of Peace." Undated.

EdTh   "Education in the Third Phase of the Industrial Era." Undated.

Fw   *Das Kreuz der Wirklichkeit, Eine Nachgoethische Soziologie.* Page proofs of the title page and a few early pages of the revised edition of *Soziologie;* vol. 1 planned for 1950 but never published.

Fy   Pages 24–73 of an untitled, undated, mimeographed fragment, probably 1940 or 1941.

LaLo   "Language, Logic, Literature." Brattle Street lecture, 20 January 1939.

LuPh   "The Luther of Physics." Brattle Street lecture, January 1939.

MePp   "Mad Economics or Polyglot Peace." 1944.

MtTt   "There Is More Time Than You Think." 1956.

ScSu   "Science, Superstition, Education and the Three Storeys of a University." Undated.

SoLa   "Soldiers in the Larger Sense." Comments on an address about William James entitled "A Soldier in the Larger Sense." Undated.

TiLe   Tippett lectures. Stockton, California, 1967. Incomplete.

IN THE FOLLOWING NOTES, numbers refer to pages. Where a page has several columns, they are lettered "A," "B," etc., from left to right.

CHAPTER 1

1. C 128; OS 144; Br9 6; SR 99. Cf. Sı 527, 686ff., 757; Sıı 408f.; F 93; UM 9f.; E 504, 506f.; AG 44, 66–72, 83f.; U 143; V 323; J 44f., 56, 62f.; O 428.

   In addition to Rosenstock-Huessy, Rosenzweig, Buber, Ebner, and Ernst Michel among others are mentioned as speech thinkers (J 72f.; AG 26f.; Sı 526, 669; SR 9). Cf. [z]7–048f.

   For other references to speech thinking or thinkers, see A 661; AG 27, 37, 57f., 64f.; JD 170; Sı 61, 739. Kindred terms are "liturgics of speech" and "liturgical thinking" (AG 35, 81, 237ff.).

   Speech thinking is time thinking and hence to be contrasted with space thinking. It is primarily concerned with traject and preject in time (see below in text) rather than subject and object (inner and outer space). "Thus speech thinking belongs to a new age of knowledge, in which time concepts, not space concepts, take the lead" (AG 25f.). Cf. AG 32; V 120; Sıı 524.

2. SR 16, 18, 43, 118f.; Sı 312, 442ff., 446, 542, 721, 796; Sıı 479; AG 35, 79.

   Yet speech is a risk (*Wagnis*); it often fails (Sı 313f.; Sıı 473, 498f.; SR 10; U 314; W 73f.; F 93; J 86f.; JD 144).

3. SR 16f., 99; G 150ff.; H 26f.; Sı 420; Sıı 275, 371f.; AG 35; U 157, 312; [ay] 358.

   Higher grammar is to master time as mathematics has mastered space (Sıı 371).

   The new grammar is also called "deeper grammar" by analogy to depth psychology (U 69); "social grammar" (G 152; UM 118f.); "primal grammar" (*Urgrammatik*) (AG 29f.; J 54; Sı 762, 768, 782, 795; G 153; [ay] 358); "fundamental grammar" (*Grundgrammatik*) (V 456); "christened" in contrast to "pagan grammar" (Sı 99); "political grammar" (V 461); and other things, some of which appear below. It contrasts with logic and mathematics because it yields multiformities and inflections instead of identities and thus is more suitable for sociology (U 314; V 107; SR 9). "Grammar lets us discover the fact that different mentalities find a place in the same person" (G 244). See chap. 3 on the multiformity of man.

4. G 130f., 158ff., 167f.; Sı 58, 339ff., 357, 384ff., 389, 410f., 420ff., 754ff.; SR 98–114, 134f.; AG 83–91; I 7; U 140ff.; V 565.

   Sı 402 uses "empirical grammar" in a different sense.

5. SI 485, 794f.; G 157, 166; OR 69, 110ff.; SII 568–79, 586; SR 16f., 82f.; U
153; [b] 255f.

Why narrative should be considered a mood is not explained. U
159 uses "preterit or perfect" instead of narrative, but that seems
even less plausible as a mood. SI 758ff. recognizes only three moods.
SII 274 says that moods and tenses are inseparably connected but
omits the narrative, perhaps because there are only three main
tenses. SII 245 identifies narrative with indicative. SI 672f., 760, and
SII 243ff. present differing correlations of moods and tenses. OR 60
associates narrative with third person plural. SII 763f. gives yet another correlation of persons, moods, and tenses, making infinitive a
fourth mood and putting indicative in place of narrative. ScSu 12
correlates future, past, and present tenses with spirit, body, and soul.
J 19 correlates "we" with indicative, "it" with infinitive. AG 86 associates past indicative with "we" and passive with "it," as if passive
were a mood.

Other examples of grammatical health are: exclusiveness of vocatives and imperatives (SII 568ff.); normally using the middle voice (as
in Greek) rather than the active and passive voices (SII 575f.); and the
use of "we" rather than "I" in narratives (SII 576f.).

6. SI 371ff., 628; SII 570ff., 763f.; OR 110ff.; G 137f., 141, 154f.; AG 88f.;
H 64ff.; V 195; U 155f.; J 25f.

[v] 528f. lists the nominative last among cases and puts *Notfall*
(need case) even ahead of *Vorfall* (pre-case) (cf. SII 763).

The German for verb is *Zeitwort* ("time word").

7. H 68; SI 48; SII 275, 457, 517ff., 558; U 170f.; E 555; AG 56; C 66ff.; D
92; I 43; G 56.

Some passages nevertheless seem to confuse names and words,
e.g. G 123.

Names are an essential feature of human as distinct from animal
languages (SI 570; SII 457; I 84).

8. AG 55f.; SII 275, 420ff.; U 172. Cf. F 15; SI 52; O 460f.; C 8.

"The powers of historical life enter my consciousness across the
bridge of the name" (U 31). Cf. IR 85.

It is difficult to see how triple intersection applies to many names,
e.g. "sociology" as distinguished from "sociologist" (U 29ff.) and
names of things generally (see note 9).

SII 502f. attributes a different kind of triplicity to names.

9. I 40–45; C 8f.; E 555; IR 85f.

Names orient us because they are reciprocal (*gegenseitig*). We need
God's name to orient us and enable us to survive other attachments
in a changing world (V 514f.; SI 78f.).

Things also have names, e.g. in ritual, poetry, or fairy tales, when they are addresssed as persons (I 41, 44; OR 87; Sᴵᴵ 532f.; O 723; Sᴵᴵ 459; AG 59). Otherwise they are merely named by people but do not answer (Sᴵ 755).

Some passages (e.g. Sᴵ 180; Sᴵᴵ 310; U 204) distinguish between geographical concepts and geographical names, the latter being associated with time, history, faith; but it is not clear how such names fit the criteria stated above.

D 103 also associates names of things with human history.

10. Sᴵ 319ff., 415, 459f.; Sᴵᴵ 577f., 586; SR 17ff., 51ff., 59, 129, 188ff.; G 149–59; U 268, 274, 280f., 295, 300; I 55ff.; Fw 15f.; C 48, 55, 166–76.

"The Cross of Reality ... is so self-evident ... that it is apt to seem trivial at first. But our 'natural' minds deny this ... truth .... It follows that the Cross is not trivial. It contradicts the abstract mentality of the 'onlooker'" (C 168).

The Cross of Reality represents "the process in which all groups are formed and maintained." "The" denotes a common pattern in the groups, not a particular "thing" (U 298, 306; J 73).

U 157 correlates "you," "I," "we," "it" with four steps of experience (*Erlebnis*): "ensoul in hearkening, inspire in communicating, hold in ascertaining, comprehend in a system."

Sᴵ 461ff. and SR 128ff. correlate parts of speech (verb, adjective, pronoun, noun) with the directions of the Cross of Reality. SR 188 lists verbs, adjectives, nouns, numerals.

I 55f. uses *fiativum, subjectivum, perfectum, abstractum* as equivalents to preject, subject, traject, and object. U 287 and Sᴵ 93 indicate correlation of the four directions of the Cross of Reality with the senses of smell, hearing, touch, and vision. Sᴵ 86ff. correlates them with drama, music, architecture, and painting.

U 310 describes a "Cross of four times." V 142 speaks of "that efficacious cruciformed time, whose fourth, dead, externalized dimension covers only the abstract time of physicists and clocks."

The Cross has a center (*Mitte*) as well as four arms. The center is the "point from which our crossings spring," "the cross switch," "the cross road," the interchange through which we pass from one arm of the Cross to another (U 295ff.; LaLo 4; cf. Sᴵ 320). It is the place of speaker or listener (SR 51, 57).

"Cross of Actuality" might be a better translation, reflecting the flavor of the German *Wirklichkeit* (cf. AG 40).

"The cross of grammar" and "the grammar of the cross" seem to be related terms (Sᴵᴵ 878f., 881, 887).

11. C 14f. Cf. C 202; EC 12.

12. MM 4; SR 11ff.; Sᴵ 445f.; Sᴵᴵ 465–79; OR 10ff.; C 173.

C 48f. gives a different view of war. AG 28 lists economic crisis instead of anarchy. V 90f. gives a different view of war and revolution.

13. G 131, 246f.; H 64f.; Sɪ 79f.; Sɪɪ 552f.

Some passages add numbers as a level lower than concepts (Sɪ 639, 648f.). Others list numbers instead of concepts (Sɪ 48, 67).

Other hierarchical expressions are high–low, above–below, degree, rank, floor. Thus, names occupy the upper story, words the ground floor, concepts the basement (Sɪɪ 552, 627; V 73, 443; G 247; AG 53, 56f.).

Sɪɪ 627 speaks of "before and after, inside and outside, above and below," as if the latter pair constituted a third axis of the Cross of Reality.

14. U 17ff., 21f., 35, 37f., 41f., 54, 56f., 178f.; G 86, 158; WA 9ff., 252, 285f.; MM 34; UM 142f.; H 28, 49, 79; Sɪ 721, 803; A 658; V 656.

"... all genuine speech remakes both listener and speaker" (C 128). The sociologist and his subject matter influence and change each other (U 34f.).

Contrary to Aristotle, Aquinas, and Rousseau, language is not part of man's natural equipment, nor is it to be known as an "object" of the natural sciences (Sɪɪ 812ff.).

15. AG 20, 64ff.; I 69, 117; J 98, 101; LaLo 11; G 119, 172, 281f.; O 733; V 132f.; Sɪ 410f.

For Rosenstock-Huessy, "grammatical forms are approached as religious revelations" (Sɪ 29).

CHAPTER 2

1. SR 183f.; Sɪ 732f.; Sɪɪ 543f.; U 198, 287f.; H 46f. Cf. C 97; TiLe 41f.; AG 165; U 35; V 329, 514, 628; G 289; J 118; SR 181.

Sɪɪ 425f. calls this argument based on language a "metanomic" (sociological) proof of God's existence, as distinguished from a proof presented to one individual. "God does not remain God, rather He becomes a mere object, when a solitary person wants to comprehend Him." (Cf. G 280.)

Though God is omnipresent, He can also be absent, notably from theology classrooms, where professors speak about Him as an object (U 307; H 46f; cf. Sɪɪ 769f.; AG 278). The contrast is clearer in German: *Gegenwart* vs. *Gegenstand*.

2. O 723–28; C 96, 184; Sɪ 42–47, 51f., 54, 57, 64f., 172ff.; Sɪɪ 656; A 13f., 103f., 716; U 10; V 633; UM 100; [z]19-1080; TiLe 41f.; G 283ff.

"Even the Bible says that our God rules over these gods" (Sɪ 45).

God's still voice is to be contrasted with Zeus, who "was never allowed to be thought of as weak, gentle, inconspicuous." "The chief god of Olympus was deprived of his freedom by his power compulsion" (SII 769).

Gerichten Gottes, judgments of God in history, as in the collapse of Germany in 1918, may be examples of God's compelling (AP 5, 63, 69; JD 188; [v] 527; [e] 10f.).

I am unable to interpret the statement that God is *offenbar* (manifest), the gods *geheim* (secret), unless it means open vs. closed to our entreaty; also that gods "make us grow silent" in contrast to the statement that we must invoke them (G 283; SI 175).

3. C 92–97, 173; G 292. Cf. SII 282, 769f.; H 46, 117; A 658.

As the Scholastics said, God is *actus purissimus*, i.e. "time without space, the most tremendous, purest verb" (D 110; U 169). Cf. D 107; SI 372; A 757.

Compare *Strom Gottes*, God's stream (A 104).

God is *unbegreiflich* (incomprehensible) because He is above us. We look down at a *Begriff* (concept), look up to His name. "Thought pulls beneath itself what it wants to comprehend" (SI 288).

"Of the people who believe that they believe in God, only a few believe in the Living God. And many believe in the Living God although they claim not to believe in God" (G 278).

"Give me one convinced atheist instead of a thousand lukewarm nominal Christians! For I can renew faith for him, but it suffocates in the thousand" (AG 288).

4. E 479; G 292; V 567; SII 135, 298, 499f.; H 24, 188; SI 53, 750; SR 141f., 185f.; J 12; TiLe 8; [bb] 196.

5. G 285–90; H 116, 168f., 177, 187, 203; C 97; SII 83, 243, 434, 758; O 727; A 103f.; V 127; JD 182; D 60; SI 170, 306; UM 134.

I am unable to interpret several striking passages relating God's creativity to his *Leiden* (suffering) or *Leidenschaft* (passion) except as they may refer to Christ's passion or to the overcoming of death generally (H 145; G 282, 292; D 105). Possibly related is *Gott gebiert* (God gives birth) (SII 575).

The doctrine of degrees of aliveness is the same as that of the five "spheres" (expounded at length in H) and the "spectrum of times" (H 156ff.). See chap. 7.

6. H 68, 182f.; V 240ff., 294; SI 56, 173ff.; SII 769; J 104; U 307.

7. SI 173–82, 192; [n] 83ff.; AG 64. Cf. V 426, 429; G 284, 292.

"Polytheism is a thousand times truer than deism or atheism" (SII 274).

The relation of the rebirth of gods to the revival of tribalism (chap. 16) is not clear.

See A 714ff. for a negative view of modern polytheism in the form
of cults and "isms."

8. V 239f., 242f.; SII 902f.; C 105; G 280. Cf. SI 466; PR 52; J 39.

Many striking passages on the Trinity are puzzling. For example:
relating it to the three tenses of time or to beginning, middle, and end
(E 520f.; G 129ff.; C 97f.; IN 10; TiLe 59f.), to the three persons of
grammar (AG 62, G 280f., SI 377f.), to faith, hope, and love (TiLe 36;
SII 135, 426; C 111), to creation, revelation, and redemption (J 14; SI
142), and to times, history, language (J 9, 14). Another passage attributes trinitarianism to Israel as well as to Christianity ([t] 206ff.). God
is alive because he is triune (D 60; G 281; SR 43). Personality has to
be attributed to the Holy Spirit because of its "temporal and topical
distinctness, concrete efficacy" (AIII 127).

9. SI 68–71, 79, 116; U 199; SII 286, 307ff., 546f., 756; V 514f., 530; JD
181–94; O 513; AG 26. Cf. H 61.

The Psalms are the primal prayers of Israel and also one form of
prayer in Christian churches to this day (AG 68; JD 180).

Prayer is the opposite of science: passionate not dispassionate
speech (JD 184f.).

I am unable to interpret SII 549 about prayer.

10. G 256; V 578; O 189f.; A 715f.; AIII 113; U 191; AG 75, 87.

11. H 116, 185f.; UM 74; G 41f., 258f., 262f.; SI 652f.; V 141f., 625; U 123f.,
218f.; AIII 113.

12. H 115ff., 186; SII 189; V 141, 598; RI1 46–49; U 109, 126; G 62.

13. SII 761; RI1 48; H 116.

CHAPTER 3

1. UM 70ff., 82ff., 118f.; SI 781.

2. U 81, 243ff., 272f., 288; V 215f.; G 59, 62; UM 52ff., 88.

Where factories run in shifts, there are also time molecules composed of three people who replace each other during twenty-four
hours (UM 52f., 55f.; C 16f.).

See the discussion of small groups in chap. 16.

The conception of "society" as composed of "individuals" derives
from the influence of natural science and natural law jurisprudence
(A 698–702). Society does not "consist" of individuals like a box of
matches. Individuals reach beyond society, and most people are not
true individuals but "bundles of nerves" (G 62).

3. UM 70ff., 83, 88, 92.

Yet UM 57 calls small factory groups collectives.

Calling a collective "all" or "infinity" is puzzling (UM 75, 105).
4. UM 82ff., 106f.; U 250f.

Expansion of the dual to include friendships, enmities, business firms, callings, families, causes, wars, revolutions, Christ and His Church, God and devil, and a statesman and his country requires qualifications or explanations that the texts do not supply (UM 83, 85f., 96f., 106; U 250f.).

Vereinzigen der Binität (making the double single) seems related to the dual (V 436f., 469f.), as does *Totenliebespaar* (couple that loves beyond death) (H 92ff.), but just how is not clear. V 752f., 755 uses *Binität* in a different sense, though perhaps also related, as it concerns the sexes.

Another instance of the grammatical method: the dual relates to the comparative (UM 84), to match the collective as superlative (see above in text).
5. UM 104ff.; U 251f., 316f.; G 286; I 119f.; SI 774f. Cf. AP 8. See chap. 4.

[bc] 291 applies the singular to the Church, which is elsewhere called a collective (UM 89) and also to *Gesellschaft* (society), also in V 760; H 39f. Cf. U 247.
6. UM 70, 86–96, 105, 108ff.; U 247f.; O 186, 724; SI 160; SII 255.
7. UM 21; D 63f.; C 115; V 633; SI 732; SR 63, 184f. Cf. SII 811.

C 114f. says that "the story of salvation on earth is the advance of the singular against the plural" and that the third millennium of the Christian era will have to "establish Man, the great singular of humanity."

On the tree metaphor see also SII 112f., 144; V 615; O 526. That metaphor seems to imply unity growing out of the past rather than only achieved in the future, but D 63 and O 526 speak of grafting, which may be a clue. See SII 112f. and V 524f. on the Jews as *Herztrieb* in this connection.

CHAPTER 4

1. SI 796ff., 772–76, 744, 295f.; A 108; UM 112f.; I 23; SoLa 17–22; H 27.

"We call 'soul' the power which can tower over our torn-to-pieces-hood between contradictory tendencies in us" (RI3 17).
2. SI 767; SII 586, 578; V 646; SoLa 1; AG 65, 76; C 17, 129, 228, 231.

I am unable to interpret "pains of death create the soul" and the related discussion of Buddha, Lao-tse, Abraham, and Jesus (U 221–25). C 174ff. gives a different view of the latter.

I am also unable to interpret "a soul is born in the growing pains of suffering in action" (C 228).

3. SI 778f., 792, 767f.; EdSt 12; AG 65; C 231; [b] 256f.; HK 26f.; SII 289, 578, 901; [k] 251; I 21; H 27; V 647f.
4. UM 113; U 213, 221, 224f., 234; H 27, 97; SII 434, 436, 530, 676; G 158, 259; [h] 69A; W 72; J 98; SI 609; A 108f.

"In times of crisis, the term 'soul' signifies our power to survive mortal fears" (I 23).

"The soul is the heart that beats beyond my body," "our power to penetrate before and after our own lifetime" (SI 19, 398).

Some passages speak of the soul of a people, a nation, a class, a science, and even the human race (SI 784; SoLa 8, 15; RI1 69; H 42; V 265). It is sometimes difficult to relate such passages to those about souls of individuals.

Israel and the Church are immortal (SII 71). Peoples are immortal in the Christian era ([bc] 285). Perhaps the clue lies in the definition of ensoulment as "one's ability to survive the death of what was one's temporary form of appearance" (H 27). Groups can be ensouled in that sense. H 27f. also applies this definition to thought (when it has the power to survive despair) as well as to marriage, people, and working group. That may also be the real meaning of SII 72f., when it says that "soul and immortality are merely two names for the same thing." C 68f. says that by anticipating death, "any form of society can attain immortality."

5. SI 19, 652f., 775, 796; SoLa 23, 28ff., 37f., 39; G 288; U 221; V 239, 274, 628, 648f.; UM 112f.; Fy 69; I 70.

This quotation evidently relates the soul to the forward arm of the Cross of Reality. Cf. U 213ff.

A dead soul is predictable, gives rise to nothing new (SII 901).

6. SI 106f., 115, 206, 454, 637, 767, 801; SII 396; AG 56; A 701; V 513.
7. V 337f., 387f., 647.
8. V 647; O 186, 724, 742ff.; SI 160, 484f., 774f., 801, 805ff.; U 304, 318, 321; I 23; ScSu 12f.; SII 253ff., 274.

AG 9f. denies the separation of mind and body because language is both. SI 482 presents mind and body as "two processes of the soul that balance each other." SI 799f. and O 186f., on the other hand, assert the Christian view that mind or spirit, unlike soul, is suprain-dividual. (The German *Geist* means both mind and spirit.) O 86 takes yet another view.

U 287 correlates soul, mind, body, and role with preject, subject, object, and traject of the Cross of Reality, saying that each takes the lead at different times.

SII 113 describes body, mind, and soul, respectively, as "our depth, the summit of our being," and "a center, the heart-shoot that drives body and mind apart and leads them together again."

SoSu 12 correlates spirit, body, and soul with future, past, and present tenses.

9. Sɪ 752, 756, 761, 802ff.; C 10; Sɪɪ 578f.
10. AG 32; G 130, 141; Sɪ 199f., 628, 782, 786f.; O 723f.; V 294, 712; I 26, 29, 110f.; SoLa 21, 26; H 25.

AG 57 confusingly calls all three vocatives, not nominatives.

The themes of the first, second, and third millennia of the Christian era are God, world, and man (V 633f.).

Sɪ 48, 80 relates God, man, and world to names, words, and numbers. G 137f. and V 137 relate them to the times spectrum with its different degrees of aliveness (chap. 7).

The world comes to self-knowledge through man (Sɪ 448).

I am unable to intepret the passages that say that man is responsible for the destiny (*Bestimmung*) of the world (V 305; HK 265; O 342. Cf. O 221; V 759; HK 253).

11. SoLa 31; TiLe 49; O 719; A 99f., 107ff., 831f.; Sɪ 202, 670; U 221; V 294, 582; C 68, 108ff., 130. Cf. V 383; Sɪ 615; AG 45.

Through nihilism, man will participate in his own further creation; God creates out of nothing (V 626, 746f.).

CHAPTER 5

1. UM 86f.; E 396; U 184.

O 50 takes a different view of individualism.

"... children do not understand the ardor of love, and ... it is useless to enlighten them about sex before they are seized by love itself .... Sex never explains love" (V 609). Cf. U 151.

2. V 514, 637, 748, 751; A 970f.; Sɪ 94, 633; Sɪɪ 591; G 88; IV 18; U 132–38.

"'Real' always is more comprehensive than any biological segment .... This fact that there is a contradiction between our physical equipment as merely male or female ... and our ambition to be human ... is at the bottom of politics and religion" (SR 156).

"Soul and mind are generalizations of woman and man" and "church and state are higher powers (*Potenzen*) of soul and mind" (UM 142). Cf. A 931.

Typical family members, daughter, son, mother, father, are also correlated with arms of the Cross of Reality (U 295; J 29; Fy 32) and with society, people, church, and state (V 105).

The European revolutions exemplified "the primal elements of the whole human soul": Italian—mother; German—father; Austrian—daughter; English—man; French—woman; Russian—son (E 547).

Some passages say that novelty and change are masculine, loyalty and perpetuity feminine (U 116; IV 32; I 85; OR 125). Others say the opposite (O 356; [an] 363).

Homosexuality is discussed chiefly in connection with Plato and ancient Greece (V 509ff.).

3. HK 254ff.; U 255ff.; V 368f.; SII 48, 486f., 490f.; I 122f., 129f.; UM 121.
4. SI 238, 714f.; SII 111ff., 118; V 367f., 513, 609, 744f., 748–55; U 274f.; O 617.

In Goethe, "masculine and feminine counterbalanced each other ... full of love and strong in faith" (D 84).

Transmission of heritage from father to daughter is particularly close (W 49; V 753f.).

I find the discussion of *how* women may acquire men's space affinities confusing (V 750ff.).

5. V 744f.; HK 273f., 284ff.
6. U 246f., 249; I 121ff.; SII 447, 585. Cf. A 699.

Today girls tend to look on themselves as boys who will become independent breadwinners. This makes for a tepid kind of homogenized love, a "homosexuality of soul" (V 510ff.).

I am unable to interpret V 754 concerning mental jealousy of wives today.

Polygamy is discussed chiefly in connection with Islam (V 374, 377, 647).

7. MM 57ff.
8. A 929ff.; O 469.

This applies primarily to love marriages since 1800 A.D. Medieval marriage was sacramental in theory but clan marriage in practice, and modern marriage beginning with Luther was dominated by the man's vocation and left only a subordinate role for the woman (A 683–86, 931, 935).

9. U 258; O 8; V 76, 282, 295; SI 190; [gy] 18; SII 143f., 147ff., 161, 811, 830ff.; EdSt 7f.; C 181f., 188f., 218ff., 223f.; A 10–15, 25.

"History can never be made by one generation" (V 271).

10. E 514; U 259, 315; SII 77, 148f., 157, 299; V 282, 310, 714f.; [gy] 18ff.; SR 12; K 202; C 37; I 124; EdSt 7f.

CHAPTER 6

1. U 234f.; O 652; SII 373, 384, 404f., 410–14; SI 390f.; V 70, 759; TiLe 30, 32f., 36f.; G 263; D 71f.; AG 44f.

I am unable to interpret much of O 648–53 regarding faith, hope, and love.

U 290, V 84, and RI3 35f. relate faith, love, and hope differently to past, present, and future. O 225f. relates hope to the future, faith to the past. U 217f., 229f. takes a different view of love. Primal grammar correlates faith, love, and hope with I-, you-, and it-sentences as modulations of one life process (AG 30, 32). Faith, love, and hope are also correlated with throat, heart, and eye (AG 28f.).

2. JD 193f.; O 653; E 396, 460f.; H 80; C 111; U 101, 182ff., 216f.; V 564, 609; RI3 23; SI 759; SII 405; J 20.

See chap. 5, note 1.

Love belongs to sphere 4, will to sphere 3, of the degrees of aliveness discussed below in chap. 7 (H 169f.).

U 136f. takes a different view of love and will.

It is well to distinguish *eros* and *agape* as a Swedish author (Nygren) has done, but *agape* is not an exclusively religious or Christian notion; it is "a fact of our soul" testified by everybody's daily experience (JD 193). Contrast SI 244f.

Some passages associate or even identify loving and naming, e.g. V 329, 629f., 649; J 57.

3. I 29; SI 391f., 649; SII 892f.; U 234; V 504; TiLe 34.

Hope radiates out into the world from us. In faith our Creator comes to His creatures to complete their creation (SI 893).

4. C 52f.; TiLe 36f.; SII 374, 408, 410, 414; A 91. Cf. RI3 33.

"We use the word faith rightly in all instances where people of different thinking and convictions cooperate ... though this faith is reflected in their brains in completely different concepts and words" (RI1 8).

AG 44f., G 226, SII 893, V 652f., 655, 709, indicate correlation between faith, love, and hope and God, man, and world. See chap. 4.

5. SII 374f., 888; RI1 49, 51; RI3 33; SI 484f. Cf. SII 135; V 649; L 8; G 290f.; AG 32f.

Bodies of time are the periods into which we bind the fleeting moments of time, as discussed below in chap. 7.

"... the Word becoming flesh is the dominant truth of Rosenstock's writings. He seeks to serve it" (UM 10). Cf. AG 14.

6. J 57; V 249, 700; G 24; SII 657; [bb] 193, 198; AG 14, 18, 34; SI 484.

7. J 57; SI 384ff., 391f., 420, 440ff.; SII 779f.; OR 49f.; AG 7, 9f., 63; SR 135.

Bodies of time are also created through language (U 314; C 167).

"Life has bodily form .... As the highest embodiment of life, as the heartbeat of love, the breath of the spirit, the image of hope ... speech blesses us with life" (AG 64f.).

"Speech is the body of the spirit" (SI 806).

These are further illustrations of speech thinking (chap. 1).

8. C 108ff., 116ff., 147f., 190; Sɪɪ 444f., 896f.; FL 133.

I am unable to interpret Sɪɪ 444 concerning the Resurrection.

CHAPTER 7

1. Sɪ 186, 194ff., 320, 395f., 470f.; Sɪɪ 627f.; SR 16, 18, 21; U 288f., 299f.; AG 46f.; V 53; O 137; I 63.

The two times and spaces of the Cross of Reality apply only to human life: "We humans are the authorized carriers of reality." Animal life differentiates inner and outer spaces. Rocks belong to only one quadrant of reality: external nature (U 131). Cf. C 166ff.; SR 17; V 19, 302; Sɪ 541, 564, 690.

There is a sense in which it is legitimate to speak of time as one. *Makroanthropos "Mensch"* (macro-"human") does become the carrier of whole-time "in the three time-binding currents of faith, love, and hope" (V 89). Sɪ 199 speaks of "the fullness of whole-time," "the unity of all times," and "the singular time." See also Sɪ 200.

Human times are not measured by instruments. They have "the qualities of living creatures" (V 737). Cf. U 166.

2. D 96f.; V 18, 342f.; U 57f., 286; I 60f.; SR 21; J 13; Sɪ 201f., 690; Sɪɪ 372, 374f., 523f., 629; C 72, 166ff.; EdTh 3.

This paragraph is another example of speech thinking.

Language is "the political power by which we establish times and spaces first of all" (Sɪɪ 372).

3. V 720, 734, 760, 50, 85, 116, 306; I 92; O 185, 457; G 169, 172, 178; U 204, 293, 315, 329; Sɪ 186, 194, 501f.; AG 25f.; E 457; RI1 1, 5. Cf. U 240f., 293.

"Dimension" is primarily a spatial term. When applied to time, it is a metaphor (SR 27f.).

Mathematics is concerned with nature, grammar with society (time) (SR 44).

See chap. 1, note 1, for the relationship of the priority of time to speech thinking.

4. V 122–27, 727; I 91–95, 101, 114. Cf. H 16f., 140, 182, 214.

5. U 95, 288; Sɪ 321, 636f., 700; Sɪɪ 243ff., 248, 257, 371, 373, 417; G 29; D 37; V 124ff., 306, 308, 385, 747f.; RI1 14f.; RI3 33f.; C 61, 123, 166; H 77f., 188; IR 130; EdTh 2f., 6ff.; SR 16; E 137; I 93f.; MM 20f.

V 125 speaks of the present as rising upwards from the waterfall of time, thus introducing the vertical dimension (chap. 1).

V 540 ascribes what seems to be a different kind of polarity to past, present, and future.

6. H 156–215; V 24–30, 132–39; G 284, 290f.; U 200; Sɪɪ 296.

The texts do not use the term "religion" for sphere 5, but they evidently mean it, e.g. when speaking of Saturn, Jahveh, and Christianity, and of *Unheil-Heil* (disaster-salvation) (H 174–76).

G 137f. distinguishes only three degrees of aliveness and describes them differently.

SI 412ff. distinguishes four degrees of aliveness, plus *unlebendig*.

V 24ff. and G 173f. apply the times spectrum to architecture.

7. V 57–91; I 69–76, 104f.; SI 62f., 183f.

Many details in these passages are puzzling and the lists of twelve vary, but the broad outline is clear.

The commands apply primarily but not exclusively to one particular time of life (I 74).

V (80f., 83, 88) relates each group of four to the Cross of Reality.

8. A 103f.; SR 181; SI 372, 472, 491f., 695f.; SII 277; D 110; J 14; CE xviii f.; C 90f.; U 248; V 141f.; H 175f.; FL xviii f. Cf. SI 198ff.; G 166.

"God is not always, for He is eternal. To be eternal He must die and rise (*auferstehen*). A dead stone is 'always'; only he who can survive death has eternal life .... Eternal precisely means not 'always' but 'always again'" (U 307). Cf. SI 56.

V 137 describes "full time, God's time, His 'always and at any time'" as the white light refracted in the times spectrum.

V 628 speaks of the "fixed point God, who lives all times in one."

Eternity is "the unity of all times" (SI 198); it is not timeless (FL xix).

9. U 308, 166; SI 471; V 121, 175, 220; E 32; G 41f.; SII 689.

Holism pervades the writings of Rosenstock-Huessy and is reflected in such terms as whole, gestalt, entire (*gesamt*), higher unity, system, field of force, organism, structure, body of time, and division of labor (U 124, 268; EC 19; SI 504ff., 744; L 39; UM 29, 96; E 32f.; MePp 15).

He sees four decades of his own life as a four-act drama corresponding to the four phases of the Cross of Reality in which "a whole is happening" (J 86). Cf. 88f.

He stresses revolution rather than gradual change because a new social order must begin all at once; then it can evolve in detail. A tribe cannot "evolve" into an empire, for example (V 175, 191, 441, 533, 556, 558; [bm] 123; H 177; O 466f., 472f.; E 158; WA 254).

Grammar likewise must work from wholes which lend meaning to the parts, contrary to the Alexandrian grammarians, who held that letters explain words, words sentences, sentences chapters, etc. (SI 36f.).

CHAPTER 8

1. AP 70ff.; V 321ff., 334, 376, 478; SII 498.

Such seems to be the meaning of "the true tribe" (V 334ff.).

Rosenstock-Huessy says that the Indo-Europeans and the Mexican Indians were mixtures already. But one passage suggests that the California Indians were purely tribal (V 156, 478ff.; SII 480, 682).

Eskimos are dismissed as paralyzed deviations, as are most of the peoples studied by ethnology today (V 362ff.).

Since the primeval tribes were prehistoric in that they left no written records, it is not clear how we are supposed to know about them, except by excavations of burial sites or through other peoples who encountered them and did keep records, as the Romans did. A number of passages, e.g. V 159, 164, 336ff., do cite observations by modern ethnologists.

2. V 155f., 158ff., 166f., 172, 202, 206ff., 334, 354; SII 480ff., 556; C 93; I 121, 123.

"The oldest language in history is mourning for the dead" (G 87).

Animals have languages of a sort, but they do not use names (SI 570). This is another respect in which human life begins with tribes. (Cf. OR 86f.)

3. V 160ff., 171ff., 204, 325, 330, 341, 354ff., 409; I 121, 129ff.; SII 486f.

V 370 and SII 486f. speak of tribal orgies as a safety valve comparable to prostitution, but I 128f. and V 46 say they resulted in marriages.

To move through jungle and bush, tribesmen used trails made by animals, who thus oriented them in space as did their ancestors in time (V 168–71).

Tribal warriors were equal; there was no hierarchy of classes or division of labor. In this respect, fascist "black shirts" and Nazi "brown shirts" were a revival of tribalism (V 163).

4. V 356, 359f., 371f., 379ff., 385. Cf. VII 259.

How the urge to migrate overcame concern for ancestral graves is not discussed.

Other sources of free variation (*Spielraum*) for tribesmen were their playful imitation of animals—swimming, stalking, climbing trees, etc.—and their use of clothing, even if only a loincloth. On the other hand, clothes, like tattooing, can assign lifelong roles. Tattooing, the earliest form of writing, created lifelong editions of a tribe's constitution (V 157, 360–68; SII 514f., 678, 736; I 128f.; [bba] 381).

5. *Zeitenfloss* (time raft) is also called *Nach wie Vor* (now as before) (V 163–68, 173, 176, 185, 208, 361). It is to be distinguished from *Zeitenschoss* (time womb), which is the mother tongue, including the names

of hero ancestors, which gives birth to named warriors; but it seems akin to *Stammesschoss* (tribal womb) and *Stammeshorizont* (tribal horizon) (V 541f.).
6. V 332f., 752; D 66; SⅡ 871.

CHAPTER 9

1. V 174, 478; SⅡ 630ff., 644, 660.

They are also called "temple states" (JD 180). *Reich* is the usual German.

V 643 f. and SⅡ 708 also mention Japan, Siam, Korea, and Cambodia.

V 173–202, 390–470, and SⅡ 595–735 contain many fascinating details on Egypt not included here.
2. V 173, 177, 183, 192, 208, 379, 382ff., 432.

The change from tribe to empire must have been sudden, not a gradual "evolution"; to work successfully, the fundamentals of the new form must have come all at once. Then, of course, it could "develop" (V 175ff., 191f.; SⅡ 602f.).
3. V 173, 187f., 254, 391, 396, 405f., 409–13, 419ff.; SⅡ 683, 692, 721; C 93.

"Here time does not die. That is the new victory over death!" (V 391).

The empire's feeling about outward space is illustrated by the Roman *limes* and the Great Wall of China (V 599f.).

The market, through which novelty came in, represented the future in the empire's Cross of Reality (V 411f.).

Ikhnaton's religious revolution seems to have been an attempt to escape the "great year" shortly before it began again. It failed. (V 405f.; G 210; SⅡ 656f., 660f.)
4. V 173–81, 187ff., 385, 389, 419ff., 426; SⅡ 625f., 632f., 643, 676f., 722; G 220.

Though empires do not migrate, the *Reichsidee* (idea of empire) does get transferred, as in the *translatio imperii* from Egypt to Rome to the Holy Roman Empire (V 461ff.).

That the pharaoh was a member of the family of gods was shown by the figure of his "ka," two uplifted hands above his head; the other gods addressed him familiarly as "thou" (V 194ff., 454ff.; I 35ff.; SⅡ 729ff.)

V 400ff. describes four main epochs of Egyptian history.

Some empires were less purely empires than Egypt. China practiced ancestor worship, a tribal trait (V 478).

An emperor brought heaven to earth. The Chinese emperor was

called the Son of Heaven. A temple was a mirror of heavenly order, a pocket edition of infinity; the temple in Peking has a glorious network of paths, stairs, and doors through which processions could move like heavenly bodies (I 46; F 88; V 173, 190).

The phallic cults, connected with the flood ritual, also broke a tribal taboo against nakedness (V 183f., 368, 472).

Pyramids were like the triangular glow, misleadingly called the zodiacal light, observable before dawn and after sunset in the latitudes of Egypt and Mexico (V 417; SII 643ff.).

The priesthood, humanity's first professional class, originated to observe the stars and calculate the flood times (V 440f.; SII 692).

5. F 88ff.; SII 625, 658f., 680; V 462–70.

CHAPTER 10

1. C 184f.; V 202f., 205, 207, 209f., 293, 295, 522f., 526ff.; V 544f.; U 224; SII 850; AIII 113; O 219, 224f.

I am unable to reconcile continuation of Israel in the diaspora with the statement that Israel came to an end with the coronation of Herod and the destruction of the temple (V 271).

The Jewish function is the root cause of anti-Semitism because it relativizes all existing loyalties (C 184; V 203).

As the time axis of the Cross of Reality was stunted by the empire, the space axis was stunted by Israel (V 410).

Passages that associate Israel with the present (U 287; V 506) or the past (C 65f., 174, 181ff.) are difficult to reconcile with emphasis on the future.

The pharoah Ikhnaton, who reigned shortly before Moses, tried like Moses to escape the Egyptian eternal recurrence. Moses succeeded by means of the exodus, but that was impossible for a pharoah (V 405f.; G 191; SII 655ff., 660f.).

After the emancipation of the Jews by the French Revolution and with the foundation of the State of Israel, the Jews are no longer performing their traditional function as priests of the only still-coming God, and all men must somehow learn to perform it (V 517ff., 520, 523; AIII 113; C 188; O 219f.).

Passages that attribute this function to other or all peoples as well as Israel (V 209f., 212, 534) are difficult to reconcile with the foregoing, or with G 49.

In any case, the Jews were not the only unique people. V 471 speaks of the Greeks as "the unique [besondere] Volk of antiquity."

V 483 speaks of the Jews in the wilderness as "the distinctive age of a new form of life," which seems to exclude Abraham.

Monotheism is mentioned as an element of Judaism but not discussed in detail. It seems somehow related to creation or to emphasis on the future, but no reason is given and the rationale for the plural name *elohim* is puzzling (I 77; V 202, 206f., 449; C 65f., 184; G 49; Sɪɪ 850). Sɪɪ 738ff. ascribes a similar faith to the Persian Emperor Cyrus, who was inspired by Zarathustra.

2. V 169, 202ff., 206, 208, 211f., 386f., 423f., 526ff., 552; G 288; Sɪɪ 678, 710f.; C 93.

U 224 seems to take a different view of death.

V 540ff. says that Moses broke with the horizons of tribe and empire by switching the numbers seven and twelve, associating the tribal seven (generations) with the week, and the empire's twelve (months) with the tribes of Israel. To what extent the latter were really tribes is not discussed. Tribes used circumcision as part of their rite of initiation; Israel voided the rite by applying it to infants (Sɪɪ 798f.).

The Ten Commandments' forbidding of images was directed against Egyptian hieroglyphs (V 423).

3. V 532f., 549ff., 553ff.

4. V 552f.; C 185. Cf. V 209f., 521; O 220.

I am unable to interpret passages related to Yom Kippur (V 529f.; JD 189f.), *Herztrieb* (heart shoot) (V 524f., 527), secret (Sɪɪ 760; I 116f.), and folk soul (Sɪɪ 114).

5. JD 181; FL 2. Cf. V 530.

CHAPTER 11

1. V 224f., 232f., 386, 475ff., 482, 489–93, 496ff., 555f.; Sɪɪ 776, 783f.

Homer, like the Jews in the wilderness period, illustrated the rule that "the first stage of a new form of life is the purest." The Greek tragedians revived elements of the tribe, the philosophers elements of the empire (V 483f.).

Greeks eliminated the human sacrifices of the tribe and the priestly caste of the empire (V 234). Greek kings did not marry their sisters, and Greek temples were not inscribed with hieroglyphs (V 470ff.).

2. V 220ff., 224f., 228–35, 244f., 248f., 476, 482–87, 496–502; Sɪɪ 613f., 793ff.

Hesiod's theogony represented a partial revival of empire themes, as did Solomon's temple (V 553ff.).

3. V 225, 242f., 314, 499ff., 506, 700, 702; I 77f.

"The Greek 'concept' joins the Egyptian 'pronoun' and the 'names of the tribe' as a newly created social speech-act, but it is socially unfruitful, for no concept obligates a questioner or answerer. We make concepts ourselves" (V 516).

Substituting concepts for names was the reaction of Socrates and Plato to the abuses of Greek sophists (SI 677).

Before philosophers generalized, Greek myths treated the gods not as concepts but as "series of activities, for which the myth composed the dramatical form" (V 232; cf. 239, 242f.). A god was a "known and acknowledged spirit" (SI 182). But UM 74 seems to take a different view.

"From Homer to Parmenides the road was still open ... to a common spirit of man .... Solely after or with Parmenides did the metaphysical prison start in which subject and object, mind and body, nature and society were forever split." Such was "the mind that beginning with Parmenides seceded from the rest of the race as peculiarly Greek and is found in all sophisticated minds today," Heidegger for example (I 77f.). Cf. V 314, 506; U 168f.

4. V 212–18, 273, 277, 391, 476f.; SII 793f.

The world of the muses was a secondary world abstracted from the main one; it comprised "what can be learned about the real world without the price of blood, sweat, tears" (V 506). Cf. 216f.; SII 793.

The Greek word for school, *schole,* also meant leisure (V 213).

We have seen that tribe, empire, and chosen people were also distinguished by differing directions of love. The contrasting Greek direction of love is not clear. One might expect something like "love of leisure activities." The texts speak variously of "admiring [*bewundernde*] love," which went with colonizing (V 501), and of homosexuality and the cult of genius (V 279). Greek genius makes everything visible, and light causes unfruitfulness; hence, the Greeks' homosexual love was the necessary foundation of their cult of genius (V 505). These striking statements are not further explained. They may have a bearing on "the school of geniuses" created by Greece (V 470, 476f.). V 797 relates genius to public and to inspiration (see also CE xviii; V 233). V 507f. seems important in connecting love and genius, but hard to interpret. *Neugierde* (inquisitiveness) is a puzzling related theme (V 507, 585f.).

5. V 249, 487ff., 502f. Cf. 254, 471, 489; J 40.

The texts do not comment on the fact that ancient Greek culture did not continue until the twentieth century A.D., as did the Jews and the Chinese empire. Greek philosophy and literature were of course revived in the second millennium, and Greek mentality dominates our academic world to this day (V 477; G44, 165; I 77f.).

No comment is made, either, on the fact that there were many tribes and a number of empires but only one chosen people and one Greece.

CHAPTER 12

1. V 255f. Cf. SI 54ff.; I 115.
2. V 260, 281f.; C 61f., 66f., 73, 104f., 108, 190; SII 895f.; H 43; A 14ff.; SI 609; IN 5.

It is tempting to think that the four ways of life correspond to the four arms of the Cross of Reality. If they do, Christ might unite them from the center of the Cross, thus being the center of history. See note 8 below.

Cf. V 279f.: "the final human," "the final way of life."

"... after the birth of Christ a times womb was created, out of which the times can be entered and left again by us" (V 284).

[t] 208 says that Abraham appeared "in the center of history."
3. V 284f., 583.

The four ways of life progressed into four freedoms, e.g. Greeks into "the free realm of ideas," Israel into freedom from magic and spirits (V 248f.).

Brief allusions to the four ways of life are scattered through many books and articles, e.g. "kings, poets, prophets, priests," and "sacrifices, poems, temples, sufferers" (V 280).

How did Jesus acquire and leave aside the antique roles? SII 800ff. and V 259 give puzzling hints.
4. V 257; E 514. Cf. V 270.
5. SII 799ff., 811, 895ff..

The four gospels, "the lips of the risen Christ" (SII 816), correspond to the four streams of language (SII 799f.; V 275). They are not a "harmony" but a symphony in four movements (V 611; FL xxi). The four evangelists "change the cross of grammar into a grammar of the cross" (SII 879, 881, 887).
6. SII 803; I 115ff.

The four gospels show respectively how Jesus reversed the four paths of speech (I 118ff.; FL passim).
7. C 93; V 277ff., 173, 214–19; G 259; A 85f.; I 101.

"By freely anticipating the death of some part of their minds, ideals, old allegiances," men "conquer the compulsory total death which hunts pagans down like nemesis." "Belief in an end of the world, or 'eschatology,' is thus the very essence of Christianity" (C 68f., 71).
8. C 174–91; U 222ff.; Fy 34–46.

This seems to say that Jesus revealed the center of the Cross of Reality (see chap. 1, note 10).

It is not clear how these "four founders" are related to the four ways of life discussed above. Tribes and Greeks seem missing.

Some passages in the pages cited seem to identify Abraham with the backward front and Jesus with the forward front, e.g. U 224f.; Fy 34f.; C 187f., 190. J 73 states yet another view. I am unable to resolve the ambiguity. See chap. 10, note 1.

U 311 says that Lao-tse's seeming to be on a par with Jesus is due to the "space thinking" of U, later corrected in V.

C 174 indicates further need for Buddha and Lao-tse in the West today, as well as for Christianity in the East: "From the purity of Eastern eyes and ears we may learn to cure the destructiveness of our sciences and the feverish expressionism of our arts." "The Cross is not an exclusive symbol of the egoism of one group; it is the inclusive symbol of the reunification of man ...." (Cf. Fy 46.)

"That men separated by continents and centuries should have undertaken a complete conquest of the soul's freedom, and should have established themselves as guardians of this freedom once for ever—this commands attention" (C 175f.).

CHAPTER 13

1. V 173 f., 537 f.; SII 99f.; FL xxi; A 616.
   The Christian era is not an arbitrary single era among many in history. It makes an epoch in contrast to *all* others (FL xvii). This obviously follows from Christ's being the center of history.
   It took "a resorption epoch of about two thousand years to use up the egg white of the pre-Christian world" (V 538).
2. SII 814, 889; V 278, 288f., 292; C 33f.; D 59; O 216f.
3. C 89, 114. Cf. C 127f., 130; FL xviiif.; A 26ff., 603.
4. SII 878; Fy 44; V 277; C 63f., 75.
5. C 74ff., 108; V 582, 268f., 376; [b] 258; U 328; SI 504ff.; SII 878; I 66.
   O (453–56, 464) shows how Aristotle's doctrine of the rotation of government from monarchy to aristocracy to democracy to dictatorship was changed in the second millennium of the Christian era; the great European revolutions from the German Reformation to the Russian modified that rotation by achieving a kind of coexistence and hence possibilities of growth. "Our Era draws hearts out of the world in order to remain unfatigued, despite the recurrence of the same in the workaday routine of factories" (V 683).
   A basic law of our era, however, requires selective revivals of the

four pre-Christian ways of life, because our freedom tends to weaken us and we need their fiery zeal (V 732f.).

Discussions relating to the Christian era often speak less of the four pre-Christian ways of life and instead contrast pagan, Christian, and Jewish, holding that a prime Jewish function has been to save Christians from relapsing into paganism. Paganism thus seems to cover elements of tribe, empire, and Greeks, but the relationship is not made clear (e.g. C 184 ff.; O 216f., 224; G 47f., 53ff.; V 295; J 72; SII 112ff., 120; E 383f.; [bc] 294f.; A 776). At other times, "pagan" seems simply to mean "Greek" (I 66f.).

EC 1 distinguishes pre-Christian paganism, which contained germs of Christian life, and "completed paganism," which occurred inside the Christian era, e.g. the Germanic gods.

6. C 75ff., 84.
7. C 61f. Cf. A 85ff., 90; C 10, 65.
8. V 573f., 419ff., 568ff., 611; SI 54, 403; SR 161.
9. F 69; G 69; V 327f.; SI 282.
10. U 174; G 127f.; SI 46f.; SII 897f. Cf. 447.

Does O 738 mean that translation implies a universal language of more than names?

SII 802f., 898f., 447; AG 14; and J 101 (on overcoming death, the Word becoming flesh, and "fruits of the end as germs of the future") should somehow fit in here.

11. UM 106; C 131, 114; H 29.
12. V 278ff., 633f.; C 114ff., 119; A 107; [bc] 290f.

"Of course this succession of epochs in the history of salvation is only partly correct. For all truths of the faith were completely given with the coming of Christ" (H 37).

A (766, 776–84) distinguishes pre-, co-, and post-churchly forces. Yet the Church is not limited to the first millennium but runs through all three (chap. 16).

Some passages correlate the three millennia with faith, love, and hope, sometimes in conflicting ways (V 282, 652, 709; H 37); with migrating from, through, and into the world (C 124); with God, world, and men (C 114); with eternity, space, and times (V 308f.; but C 20 puts time in the singular, "God's one time"); with saints, revolutionaries, and nihilists entering heaven, purgatory, and hell (V 624f.; cf. H 50; BeAf 61f.); with the articles of the Creed: redemption, creation, and revelation (C 115f.); with conversion, reformation, and incarnation (C 120ff.); and with the disciplining of bodies, minds, and souls (V 743f.; but 646f. puts them in a different order). V 633 seems to correlate the millennia with three reconciliations: the self-reconciliation of God (or reconciliation of all times—the connection is obscure), the reconciliation of things in the world, and the reconciliation of hatred among men.

The first millennium inherited Israel; the second, Hellas and Rome (and competed with other ancient empires); and the third millennium is to revive aspects of the tribe (V 311f., 680f., 683f.; cf. A 487, 489f.). SII 158f. offers a kindred but somewhat different view.

Not all themes correspond to millennia, however. For example, Church history so far falls into four periods of 500 years each: soul church, culture church, mind church, and nature church (evidently corresponding to the Cross of Reality as described in U); see G 39ff.; A 668; AIII 116f. Similarly, the four stages in the history of the schism between Western and Eastern churches are 500 years apart (C 138ff.). The second millennium is often divided into medieval and modern periods (e.g. SII 57), and its universities are correspondingly Scholastic, then academic, to be followed by "argonautic" in the third millennium (e.g. V 683ff.).

I am unable to interpret "the soul is ever more exclusively the source and guarantee of all knowledge in the Christian era" (A 671).

CHAPTER 14

1. V 619, 646–48; A 107ff. Cf. A 766.
2. C 114f.; V 278, 618; A 82f., 90, 107; H 29.
   Conversion is presumably the meaning of establishing one God in place of many false gods (C 114; H 29).
3. V 279, 284–87; A 85.
   Cf. A 13f.: the Church as Proteus, ever new.

   Protestantism was wrong in regarding the early centuries as decadent compared to primitive Christianity. The Holy Spirit has to change its forms of expression as it unites succeeding generations in one Spirit (SII 831f.).

   Members of the Church "do not die in order to die. They die because they let the call of the future become master of all the past" (A 89f.).

   The Church perpetuated Jesus' attainment of success through renunciation of personal success, thereby achieving "a coherent effectiveness for all times of a people and for the peoples of all times" instead of a meaningless ebb and flow (A 11–16, 30).
4. V 287, 289–95; C 118ff., 124; A 106.
   The correspondence to the Cross of Reality is evident. Likewise the "four authorities of liturgy, papacy, theology, and monasticism,"

which "are the essence of what the Church is": they overcome the four "fortresses of life" built by Jerusalem, Rome, Athens, and Egypt (A 92–102).
5. V 595–619; C 119.
    V 618 hints at a correspondence between the four saints and the Cross of Reality.
6. V 613; A 602f., 667f.; C 120.
    The Church of the first half of the first millennium was a soul church, of the second half a culture church, bringing treasures of civilization to the barbarians (G 39).
7. C 152ff.; G 223; A 463ff.; V 619.
    Islam is of course not part of the Christian era. It is a development of tribalism (V 373ff.).

CHAPTER 15

1. G 234; V 297f., 300, 302, 305, 650ff., 664; A 659f., 665.
    These remarks throw light on the meaning of calling the second millennium the "space millennium" (see chap. 7) and relating its revolutions to "the spaces of hope" (V 306, 308f., 639, 641, 650ff., 675; S1 203; G 226ff.). See note 3 below.
    V 298 says that the second millennium became a dialogue between Church and world (cf. A 660). V 619 says that it carried every word from the Church into politics.
    A dialogue with an indifferent world is puzzling. What do world and Church say to each other? "Dealing" with the world might be a better term. V 656 speaks of a different dialogue in world history: between revolutionary heroes.
    Though the second millennium is primarily world history, it is also a world of schools, the Scholastics of medieval universities inspired by Aristotle and the academics of modern universities inspired by Plato. Out of the latter came modern natural sciences and technology. They, along with the Crusaders and explorers, unified the world in another way (V 624, 639, 683ff., 304f.; C 114ff.).
2. G 43, 188, 204, 217ff., 230ff.; O 74, 454f., 462, 714f., 730; V 681f.; E 5.
    Thus, there is progress characteristic of the Christian era.
    Counterrevolutions conversely are not total; they speak only a partial language like that of the German racists (U 179; O 526). Fascists and Nazis were counterrevolutionaries (O 623). So were the Jesuits in the Counter-Reformation (O 161ff., 229) and the Ghibellines in Italy (V 668f.). Stalin became one (E 23, 504).
    In the second millennium, there have also been revolutions that

were not world revolutions, for example, 400 of them in medieval Italy (V 95; O 465f.; E 6).

In the future, revolution can be manipulated as a vital force for change (O 23).

3. V 653f. Cf. 635, 675.

Another term for enslavement is perhaps *die Uebermacht der Räume* (the predominance of spaces) (V 720; cf. 674). See note 1 above. E 373 says that all revolutions broke out against space thinking. Cf. E 431.

V 635 says that the second millennium consists of revolutions because the world resists the Holy Spirit. This seems to imply that the revolutionaries seek to overcome the resistance in each case.

4. E 80ff., 92; V 658; G 38.

The *wunde Punkt* (sore point), *Druckpunkt* (pressure point), *erregendes Moment* (arousing factor), or "initial impulse" seems at times to be an event (e.g. Sutri), at times an unjust situation (e.g. lack of a party of religion in England, or a shift in the basis of the emperor's power) (E 80f., 131, 139; O 530). In another case, the sore point is an early feature of one revolution that makes it vulnerable to a later one (e.g. Gergory VII's alliance with the vassals of the emperor, exploited centuries later by Luther against the pope) (E 146).

5. O 488f., 503f., 530; E 116f., 131, 133ff., 138ff.; Si 203.

6. V 44f., 640; O 506ff.; E 73, 122, 141f.

O (511, 607, 609) calls Odilo a revolutionary comparable to Hildebrand (Gregory VII) and St. Francis; and V 642 lists the emperor and Cluny as carriers of the first revolution and calls the Gregorian the second revolution (cf. V 680; O 548, 682). But this "first" revolution is not described in parallel with the rest—no pressure point, etc., and we are not told what it was against.

7. O 518, 534ff.; E 137f.

Gregory VII treated churches as points in space, thus setting the tone for the space millennium (V 301f.).

8. O 537ff., 543ff.; E 143ff., 149ff., 489.

9. O 543.

10. O 541f.; E 26, 146, 157.

Celibacy for all the clergy was made mandatory by the revolutionary popes, an important means of detaching them from local ties and hence putting them more fully under papal control (E 146; A 603f.; O 520).

11. E 31, 159f., 161f., 169.

O 595 ends arrogance in 1147.

V 642 dates humiliation from 1134.

12. E 17, 149, 169ff., 186ff., 194f.; O 564, 566, 569, 584, 587, 597.

E 554 in listing seven kinds of revolutionary spirit evidently counts the Italian and the two halves of the Papal Revolution as three revolutions.

The Italian Revolution is really a mixture of clerical and secular. E (269, 407, 548, 550ff.) seems to group the Reformation with the clerical revolutions. O (33, 453) groups it with the secular. E 380 and O 715f. say that all revolutions before the French were Christian. Yet the French and the Russian were also results of the Christian era (O 716). E 549 relates clerical and secular revolutions to time and space, respectively.

It is not always easy to tell which half of the Papal Revolution a particular passage is referring to, and sometimes there seems to be downright ambiguity. Thus E 488f. describes different eschatologies (final victory of the Crusades, the Antichrist) for each half, but O 552ff. connects the Antichrist with both.

13. O 565–71; E 173ff., 178f.
14. E 132f., 188; O 571f.
15. O 585, 588ff.; E 169ff., 181–84, 189.
16. O 595–602; E 31, 198–201, 203–6.

E 204f. and O 597f. seem to say that the Renaissance was the golden age for the whole period 1000–1500.

17. E 83, 216f., 293; O 33, 375, 378, 453.

The Reformation was a revolution against the pope, not the emperor (E 218).

18. O 572f.; E 208f.

O 369 says that Germany had sixty archbishops and bishops.

O 374 says that six bishoprics overlapped the territory of Luther's prince. O 377 lists ten; E 208, eight.

19. O 374f., 380f., 394f.; E 208f., 212f., 219–22, 225f., 242ff. Cf. E 283; O 272f., 276.
20. O 386, 364ff.; E 218f., 227ff.
21. O 364; E 31, 251–55.

E 246 uses "Protestantized" to include German Catholics; cf. 252, 546.

V 642 seems to extend humiliation to 1654.

22. E 255ff.; O 435. Contrast note 32 below.
23. O 393, 442ff.

Rosenstock-Huessy foresaw the rise of someone like Hitler, "a kaiser of lies," in 1919 (SII 109, [te] 1C).

24. E 214f., 248ff., 258; O 393f., 398f., 402, 427, 440ff.

Luther also Christianized household and barnyard and labor, which had been pagan before (A 682f., 685, 687f., 694; O 448f.).

25. E 241f., 251; O 368ff., 371ff.
26. E 243f., 247f., 251; O 404ff.

27. E 81–84, 236, 288, 290ff.; O 272f., 276, 394; G 18f.
28. O 258–61, 274, 277, 301ff., 310, 322f., 345ff.; E 281ff., 287f.; G 37.

Yet O 347 and E 288 speak of a twofold beginning or two-stage course, mentioning only the first and third phases.

Charles II carried through the parliamentarization of the Church of England (O 322). His "restoration" in fact retained many of the changes wrought by Cromwell and actually strengthened Parliament's position by disbanding the army (E 305f.).

29. E 270ff.; O 275f., 278f., 310f.
30. O 290–301, 332; E 264ff.; 302–5, 316.
31. O 261, 348–51; E 308.

O 261 dates the period of pride from 1745; but O 351 dates it from 1730, and E 31 dates it from 1714. No date is explained.

32. E 31, 272, 308f.; O 261, 349, 597.

The French and Russian golden ages might be yet to come. But E 204 and O 705 seem to imply that 1870–1914 was a combined golden age for German, English, and French revolutions. See note 16 above.

33. O 324ff., 357f.; E 302f., 273f., 315ff., 487; [ax] 114f.

Other themes connected with the English Revolution are public spirit (O 319ff.; E 295), Charles I as saint of the Anglican Church (O 318), demilitarization (E 306; O 359), the sad fate of Ireland (E 301ff.), the budget (O 280ff.), and Old Testament language (O 324ff., 330f.; E 269f.).

34. O 257f., 341f.
35. E 326, 330–34; O 164ff.
36. O 138, 152–57, 161, 166; E 293, 331f., 334, 338–44.

With the expulsion of the Jesuits from France in 1761, absolute monarchy lost its intellectual allies in its fight against Paris (O 163; E 336).

37. E 318f., 354, 369f., 379; O 178ff., 193–96, 198, 236, 248f.

Less is said about the idea of fraternity. It seems to be associated with Freemasonry, nationalism, and the cult of friendship as a counterpoise to individualism (E 351, 379; O 195).

38. E 79, 360–67, 371f., 379, 385ff., 401, 403; O 182, 213ff.

The egocentric individualism fostered by the French Revolution flowered in the cult of genius (E 385, 388f.; O 245).

39. O 132f., 135, 217f.; E 325.
40. O 133ff.; E 29, 31, 366, 386f.
41. E 344–49, 352f., 363, 373; O 176ff., 195ff., 238ff.

After World War I, another part of the unwritten constitution was government of the Catholic Church in France by Freemasons (the French government) through the papal nuncio (O 244).

42. E 381f., 384f.; O 217f., 234f.

43. O 148, 168f., 198–201, 229, 236; E 59ff., 327f., 357f., 360; G 44ff.; [bc] 291.
44. O 146f., 201ff., 211ff., 244–52; E 345f., 348, 362f., 373, 375–80, 390–93.
45. E 407ff. devotes a chapter to yet another revolution, that of the German great powers, Austria and Prussia. It is inserted between the chapters on the French and Russian revolutions. This revolution is interpreted as a secular repetition of the German princes' revolution known as the Reformation, but it does not fit easily into the European series of total revolutions. O 618ff. treats Austria fragmentarily but ignores Prussia. E 547 gives a daughterly role to Austria but mentions nothing corresponding for Prussia. E 548 omits both Austria and Prussia in enumerating six European revolutions. E 554 also omits both.

    E 94f., 264f., and O 662ff. list a number of "half-revolutions" from the sixteenth to the nineteenth centuries. They failed—each in a different way—to meet all the requirements for a total revolution: Spain, Holland, Sweden, Poland, and America. O 679 calls the American a "minimum revolution." The so-called Industrial Revolution, on the other hand, is dismissed as being not a revolution but an evolution (UM 35; O 704). However, the resulting worldwide industrial economy made possible by the science and technology developed in the second millennium has major implications for the third millennium (see chap. 16).
46. E 78ff., 404ff., 442ff., 447ff., 479; O 36–44, 90; G 220.
47. O 55f., 138; E 79f., 445f.

    A gradual redistribution of the land was planned, to be completed by 1932 (O 38f.).
48. E 450ff., 462–68; O 52ff., 61, 65ff.; V 678.
49. [te] 28B; O 65, 67; E 462f., 525, 528. Cf. IV 22f.; AP 35f.
50. E 79, 444ff., 449f., 469f., 482; O 64f.; [bm] 120f.
51. O 72f., 138, 499; [te] 28BCD; MtTt 1f., 5bf.

    MtTt 5b compares Stalin's earlier period to Napoleon, his later one to Louis XVIII and Charles X.

    E 32 says nothing about a restoration but ends the initial period in 1942 or 1950. E 504 and G 38f. say that Stalin became his own counterrevolutionary. E 23 dates Stalin's counterrevolution at 1945. There is no mention of a period of humiliation, except that V 643 gives puzzling dates and MtTt 13f. hints at something analogous to Napoleon III occurring after 1970.
52. E 3, 16, 76f., 486, 490f., 514, 524f., 539f.; O 51f., 95, 101, 103, 105; V 113, 678; [bm] 120f., [te] 1A, 1B, 1D, 28A; I 185.
53. AP 37f., 63; [te] 1B, 1D, 1E, 28A, 28C, 28D; E 3f., 15, 18, 32f., 35, 52ff., 434f., 510, 523ff., 529f.; C 4f., 51; O 254; G 38; [h] 7; H 193; SI 699f.

What is meant by structure is not explained. Perhaps it means transforming the frame of reference from Europe to the planet.

"... the World War revealed its destructive force as the end of a civilization" (O 515).

V 639 says that a third world war would be "good night to all history"—probably referring to a nuclear holocaust.

The rhythm of pride and humiliation does not seem applicable to the World War revolution (cf. V 643).

One may discern—though no passage makes it explicit—that there is a similarity between the linkage of the Papal and the Italian revolutions and that of the World War and the Russian revolutions. The papal and the World War revolutions came in two halves, and they were not national revolutions but each involved one.

O (x, 14, 485) calls the German, English, French, and Russian revolutions secular revolutions made by the secular power, and the earlier ones plus the American Revolution clerical. E 407, however, calls the Reformation a religious revolution, which was secularized later by the Revolution of the German Great Powers (see note 45 above). O 10 says that the World War "dealt with religious aspects" not represented by the secular revolutions and that America "belongs to at least three different types of revolutionary events." O 662ff. groups the American with a series of "half-revolutions" (see note 45 above). O 657–61 groups the American Revolution with a series of "precursor revolutions" that failed, e.g. the Paris Commune of 1871. In this respect, the American is considered a precursor of the French. Perhaps the third type of revolutionary event was exemplified by the World Wars (cf. O 676ff.).

54. For the French and Russian revolutions, a period variously called incubation, restoration, or reaction came between upheaval and arrogance (O 136; MtTt 5b). It is not mentioned for the earlier revolutions, though there was a possibly corresponding gap in the English rhythm (E 31). The "restoration" of Charles II in England was different, coming in the period of upheaval. MtTt 4 describes the periods differently.
55. E 83f., 218.
56. O 130f., 227, 470–75, 480.
57. E 84ff., 289; O 160.
58. E 92ff., 404.
59. O 455f., 458, 663f.
60. E 73ff.; 128f., 293, 359, 404, 416, 456; O 195f., 475, 587, 622ff.
61. E 77; O 252, 457f., 625. Cf. O 75f.
62. O 519f., 712ff., 734; E 541–48; G 232; [ax] 118f.

    E 547 and O 616–19 assign daughterhood to Austria. Nothing is listed for Prussia.

O 679–82 and E 109ff. relate these languages to second languages found in seven "sacramental orders" or evolutionary phases of creation described by Hugo of St. Victor, e.g. Noah or natural law for the American Revolution. O 711 adds pre-Adamitic forces for the Soviets (cf. 738f.). These biblical languages embed the revolutions in "world history."

63. O 24f., 50, 481, 728ff.; [ax] 115f., 119f.; E 201ff., 251, 537ff. Cf. O 256, 393.

64. O 8, 119–22, 129, 333; E 20, 168, 258, 489.

65. E 103f.; V 660f.

There is some mention of existentialists, work service, Stalin on language (cf. E 400, 503ff.).

After a revolution, there is a process of resorption, sucking up aspects of the previous heritage, as after the French Revolution and in Russia today (V 532f.).

66. O 475–79, 711f.; E 24, 478–85. Cf. O 460f., 525f.

But the spirit takes a different form in each revolution (E 554).

67. E 396ff., 485–89; O 110f., 555–59.

An eschatology for the World War revolution is only obscurely hinted at (E 490f.).

E 488f. inserts an eschatology for the Crusades, but how it fits in is not clear.

Several other generalities are suggested regarding the whole cycle of revolutions, but they are puzzling or incomplete: E (387, 554ff.) lists different kinds of spirit; E 18f. and O 347 list twofold beginnings; O 417ff. and E (189ff., 533–36) discuss music, painting, and the novel in relation to the Reformation and the Italian, English, and Russian revolutions.

68. V 639ff., 653, 670, 712ff.; E 53ff., 111, 537; D 26, 30; G 42, 233; O 714.

All social strata have had their revolution and hence all seats are taken (E 69ff.; cf. O 713f.).

69. G 43, 233f.; C 114, 131; H 29; V 650; E 537. See notes 1 and 2 above.

In the third millennium, many rhythms will pulse simultaneously through the unified world. Things will change too fast "to establish human pedigrees" (G 43, 233).

CHAPTER 16

1. S₁ 654; E 32f.; J 42; D 13, 106; TiLe 64: [h] 77Bf.; G 41ff.; V 309, 625, 639, 734ff.

[h] 68B speaks of the beginning of a Slav millennium (cf. SII 68, 84).

Rosenstock-Huessy never hints at the possibility of a fourth millennium. On the contrary, he seems to imply that the third is the last, as in such passages as "we shall enter the last era of history" (O 726), "the preliminary labor pains of the end-time shade us" (A 657; cf. V 257; H 38; Fy 63; SII 158; SI 214f.). The idea of completing a whole is also suggested by "The third millennium: man shall become complete (vollzählig)" (V 309; cf. 314, 702). The correlation of the three millennia with several groups of three, such as faith, love, and hope, implies that there is no fourth (see chap. 13, note 12).

2. C 20, 114f.; H 29. Cf. SII 446f.; V 633f.; [ea] 8f.; [h] passim.

3. V 138, 308–14, 702, 726f., 749, 760; [bba] 377–82; UM 30–51; EdSt 10; D 100f.; G 175ff.; E 514; SII 296; C 18f. See chap. 7.

I am unable to interpret V 728ff. on high times and mastering time.

"What has revealed itself successively in the fullness of times is going to unfold itself simultaneously in the fullness of the end without end" (A 657; cf. v 257; SI 214f.; SII 300).

Rosenstock-Huessy's own thought fits into this historical context as an effort to develop our rootedness in times and overcome the predominance of space (V 19).

4. V 624f., 744–56; U 131–40. Cf. [t] 218ff.

I am unable to interpret much of the discussion of nihilism in V 624ff.

5. I 121; O 715, 717f., 733; V 312, 378, 344, 731ff.; C 121f.; [bc] 294f.; SII 158ff.; [bba] 382; UM 36ff. Cf. C 40; AH 70ff., 77f.

War changes human nature and it therefore should be abolished only if a "moral equivalent" is found. Change in human nature is indispensable (C 48f.; cf. 26f.; I 31ff.)

[bc] 292f., 295 says that we need tribal means to prevent the socio-economy from making us bloodless, but how tribal means lead to abundance of blood is obscure. Perhaps this passage associates blood with warmth. [bc] 286f. connects blood with ancestry. SII 159f. speaks of blood ties. Since language is the lifeblood of society (SR 10), these passages may be referring metaphorically to the way language dies in the modern socioeconomy and needs tribal life for its rebirth ([bc] 295; V 754; C 5; I 121).

Of the four ways of life B.C., the first millennium inherited Israel, the second revived Greece and Rome and competed with other empires. Hence, the tribe remains for the third millennium to revive (V 311f., 680f., 683f.). Cf. SII 158f.

6. C 211ff.; UM 57, 60 ff., 88; WA passim; L 48ff. Cf. SI 516; A 725f.

Apparently related terms are: spiritual families as islands of intercommunication (V 740; cf. 733, 755f.); "sacramental groups," "pentecost groups" (AG 281ff., 292; G 63); "consecrated fellowships" (C 213); "binding, nonfungible groups" (G 177f.); and, less directly, *Mitarbeiterstämme*, staff cadres sent by a parent firm to establish branches (U 250f.; UM 139ff., 162, 165ff.). Sacramental groups are evidently the answer to the disintegration of groups by modern technology.

"If industry had established group tenancy of tested workers over periods from five to fifteen years, Germany might have escaped Hitlerism" (C 213).

7. C 116. Cf. H 34f.; UM 115; O 729f.
8. C 26ff., 49, 204f., 238; J 84f.; U 9f.; [f] 140–45; AH 20f., 36f., 57f.; [gy] 15; [bn] 5f., 146–60; I 30ff.; V 109; D 45–52; [gi] 36, 38; [ea] 8f. See Jack J. Preiss, *Camp William James* (Norwich, Vt.: Argo Books, 1978).

"Socioeconomy" seems the best translation of *Gesellschaft* as used here; it is described as "humanity economically connected over the whole earth in division of labor" (A 771). "Industrial society" is a kindred term (C 226).

The idea of volunteer work camp service is echoed in the section on argonautics (sociology based on experience of peace) (V 698).

9. V 714, 717, 719ff.; O 730ff.; G 220f.; [te] 1E, 28A; E 362ff.; C 161; D 64; MM 44; MePp 16f.
10. V 114, 280, 735f.; D 63ff.; H 29ff.; C 114f.; AH 53; [h] 69A, 77Bf.; A 770–75, 778ff.; O 605.

In any case, there must be no single world-state: "that would be our death," "the most abominable tyranny" (E 531; V 760).

V 103ff. gives a fascinating discussion of socioeconomy, state, church, and people as "political states of aggregation," but I am unable to interpret it.

11. C 24, 30f., 41, 100f., 126ff., 160; PR 44–55; SI 208–20, 261–65; A 710ff., 774, 780–84; H 36f.; [gy] 19f.; Fy 60, 71; AG 281; [b] 247ff., 252–60.

Rosenstock-Huessy's work with the Daimler factory magazine and the Frankfurt Academy of Labor were experiments in adult education (A 712; K 90ff.; V 311), as were his gatherings with soldiers behind the lines in World War I. His work service camps, described above in the text, were evidently intended to be examples of the Listening Church (cf. [b] 257). The Church in the coming age will be democratic rather than monarchical, will cope with the world economy rather than the state, will be less concerned with dogma and law, and will call for more participation by the layman, "the unforeseen human, who forms communities by his activity" (A 781f.).

"Sacramental groups," "families of the Holy Spirit" instead of individual saints, will renew the visible Church (AG 281ff., 292). See note 6 above.

I am unable to interpret UM 162, which seems to identify the small church groups with the staff cadres mentioned in note 6 above.

12. H 36; C 116.

CHAPTER 17

1. J 42f.; I 3–7; U 304; H 196; A 27; SI 293f.; E 489; G 168.
2. MePp 17; O 68f.; U 18, 179, 181f.; SI 293f.; UM 67.
3. O 76–89; G 221; E 404ff.

   Mechanical time is the lowest sphere in the spectrum of times (chap. 7).

4. V 113, 452, 669; [bm] 118f.; O 74f., 458, 464f., 736; E 404; G 220. Cf. E 68ff.; BeAf 43.
5. U 160, 304, 310; V 589f.; G 168; SI 233f.; SII 82f., 770f.; C 92, 97, 123; A 27ff., 771.

   U 315ff. compares Nietzsche and Descartes as representatives of the "space thinking" that has dominated modern times. But RI1 13 says that Nietzsche was the rediscoverer of the future and its logical function as a basis for present evaluations.

   I am unable to interpret SI 239ff. about Antichrist, or V 729ff. on Nietzsche's relation to times, spaces, and tribalism.

6. U 303ff., 310; G 168; AG 54.

   C 211 and J 45 expose the individualistic shortcomings of psychoanalysis. Psychoanalysts go in for loosening family ties but they do not understand binding and do not realize that loosening is for the sake of binding, not vice versa (SI 353; V 17).

7. V 258; Br9 1f.; SR 10; SI 305; SII 422f.; [v] 528; [g] 100.

   I am unable to interpret V 20 with regard to Darwin's ideas about the struggle for existence.

8. C 54ff.; BeAf 9.
9. V 16–20; BeAf 8f., 11ff. Cf. [bb] 203.
10. SII 57f., 64f., 72f., 80, 82; E 56; J 75; TiLe 22; [h] 68Aff.; A 30.

    The World War is mentioned briefly in Spengler's tabular outline of political epochs but with nothing like Rosenstock-Huessy's major emphasis.

11. SII 57ff.; SI 434f.
12. C 63; [h] 68B, 78B; SII 61f., 71f.; TiLe 22; V 284; [te] 1A.

    Rosenstock-Huessy admits some cycles in history, e.g. the Polyb-

ian rotation of government, but not as a natural law like Spengler's seasons (O 453ff., 602ff., 718).
13. [h] 69A, 77Bf.; SII 81.

One of Spengler's deepest remarks is that "every civilization sets out with a new experience of death" (O 508).

THE WRITINGS OF

EUGEN ROSENSTOCK-HUESSY

A Comprehensive Bibliography
by Lise van der Molen

EDITOR'S NOTE: Lise van der Molen is a Th.D. candidate from the Netherlands who is writing a dissertation on Eugen Rosenstock-Huessy's thought and has spent many years preparing this bibliography. It is the first comprehensive, cross-referenced compilation of all the published writings of Rosenstock-Huessy. The 457 entries are organized in four sections: Books and Pamphlets; As Editor or Co-editor; Posthumously Published Works; Articles.

Mr. van der Molen is in the process of completing an extensive "Inventory" of Rosenstock-Huessy's unpublished writings, which are located in the three Eugen Rosenstock-Huessy Archives, at Four Wells in Norwich, Vermont, in the Baker Library at Dartmouth College, and in Bielefeld, West Germany. Included in the inventory are unpublished articles, lectures, reviews, course material, sermons, poems, and selected letters. For further information the reader may write to Drs. Lise van der Molen, 't Olde Hof 22, 9951 JZ Winsum Gr., The Netherlands.

Among the unpublished works are approximately 300 recorded lectures, including those comprising the six courses Rosenstock-Huessy

155

taught at Dartmouth College between 1949 and 1957. The University of
Florida in cooperation with the Eugen Rosenstock-Huessy Fund has pro-
vided partial support for a five-year project involving the transcription
of the Dartmouth course lectures and many of those delivered at other
institutions. For further information the reader may write to Mrs. Freya
von Moltke, President, The Eugen Rosenstock-Huessy Fund, Four Wells,
Norwich, Vermont 05055.

BOOKS AND PAMPHLETS

1. *Landfriedensgerichte und Provinzialversammlungen vom neunten bis
   zwölften Jahrhundert.* Inaugural-Dissertation zur Erlangung der Dok-
   torwürde einer Hohen Juristischen Fakultät der Ruprecht-Karls-Uni-
   versität zu Heidelberg. Breslau: M. & H. Marcus, 1910. 52 pp.
   = First part of **2**.

2. *Herzogsgewalt und Friedensschutz.* Deutsche Provinzialversammlungen
   des 9.–12. Jahrhunderts, Untersuchungen zur deutschen Staats- und
   Rechtsgeschichte, begründet von Otto von Gierke im Jahre 1878. Alte
   Folge, Heft 104. Breslau: M. & H. Marcus, 1910. 205 pp. Reprint ed.,
   Aalen: Scientia Verlag, 1969.
   Includes **1** as part 1.

3. *Ostfalens Rechtsliteratur unter Friedrich II.* Texte und Untersuchungen.
   Weimar: Hermann Böhlaus Nachfolger, 1912. vi + 147 pp.

4. *Rathaus und Roland im deutschen Stadtrecht zwischen 1186 und 1280.*
   Weihnachtsangebinde für Karl Zeumer, 24. Dez. 1912. Leipzig: Hand-
   schrift der Spamerschen Buchdruckerei, n.d. 47 pp.

5. *Königshaus und Stämme in Deutschland zwischen 911 und 1250.* Leipzig:
   Felix Meiner, 1914. Reprint ed., Aalen: Scientia Verlag, 1965. xii + 416
   pp.

6. *Europa und die Christenheit.* Kempten-Munich: Jos. Köselsche Buchhandlung, 1919. 31 pp.

7. *Die Hochzeit des Kriegs und der Revolution.* Die Bücher vom Kreuzweg,
   Folge 1. Würzburg: Patmos-Verlag, 1920. 306 pp.

8. *Werkstattaussiedlung.* Untersuchungen über den Lebensraum des In-
   dustriearbeiters. In Verbindung mit Eugen May und Martin Grünberg.
   Berlin: Julius Springer Verlag, 1922. 286 pp.

9. *Zerfall und Ordnung des Industrievolks.* Frankfurt a.M.: Carolus-Druck-erei, 1923. 39 pp. Reprinted from *Rhein-Mainischen Volkszeitung* (Frankfurt a.M.).

= 10.

10. *Industrievolk.* Aus dem Zwischenraum zwischen Technik und Weis-heit, Aus der Zwischenzeit zwischen Krieg und Frieden. In der Reihe: *Volk im Werden,* Schriftenreihe der *Rhein-Mainischen Volkszeitung, 2. erweiterte Auflage.* Frankfurt a.M.: Carolus-Druckerei, 1924. 55 pp.

= 9 (expanded).

11. *Abbau der politischen Lüge.* In der Reihe: *Volk im Werden, Schriftenreihe der Rhein-Mainischen Volkszeitung.* Frankfurt a.M.: Carolus Druckerei, 1924. 81 pp.

12. *Angewandte Seelenkunde. Eine programmatische Übersetzung.* Bücher der deutschen Wirklichkeit, edited by Wilhelm Henrich. Darmstadt: Röther-Verlag GmbH, 1924. 79 pp.

Also in **46**, pp. 739–810.

13. *Protestantismus und Volksbildung.* Berlin: Eckart-Verlag GmbH, 1925. 24 pp.

Also in **57**, 2: 675–728 ("Luthers Volkstum und Volksbildung"; ex-panded version, omits final quotation from John 1: 1–5).

14. *Soziologie I. Die Kräfte der Gemeinschaft.* Berlin and Leipzig: Walter de Gruyter & Co., 1925. 264 pp.

= **39** (revised).

15. *Lebensarbeit in der Industrie und Aufgaben einer europäischen Arbeits-front.* Berlin: Julius Springer Verlag, 1926. 88 pp.

16. *Vom Industrierecht. Rechtssystematische Fragen.* Festgabe für Xaver Gretener. Berlin: H. Sack, 1926. 183 pp.

17. *Religio Depopulata.* Zu Josef Wittigs Ächtung. Berlin: Verlag Lambert Schneider, 1926. 44 pp.

Also in **57**, 3: 103–32.

18. *Unser Volksname Deutsch und die Aufhebung des Herzogtums Bayern.* Breslau: Korn, 1928. 66 pp. Reprinted in Hans Eggers (Hersg.), *Der Volksname Deutsch* (Wege der Forschung, Bd. 151) (Darmstadt: Wissenschaftliche Buchgesellschaft, 1970), pp. 32–102.

= **315**.

19. *Die ungeschriebene Verfassung.* Eine Rede zum 11 August 1928. Bres-lau: Breslauer Akademischer Verlag, 1929. 13 pp.

= **324**.
Also in **20**, pp. 32–41.

20. *Politische Reden*. Vierklang aus Volk, Gesellschaft, Staat und Kirche. Berlin: Verlag Lambert Schneider, 1929. 55 pp.

21. *Die Arbeitslager innerhalb der Erwachsenenbildung*. Stuttgart: Verlag Silberberg, 1930. 20 pp.
Reprint of **328**.

22. *Die europäischen Revolutionen. Volkscharaktere und Staatenbildung*. Jena: Eugen Diederichs Verlag, 1931. iv + 554 pp. 2 Zeittafeln.
= **35, 45** (revised).
See **28** (a different version).

23. *Revolution als politischer Begriff in der Neuzeit*. Breslau: M. & H. Marcus, 1931. 41 pp.
Reprint of **336**.

24. *Kriegsheer und Rechtsgemeinschaft*. Rede, gehalten zur Verfassungsfeier der Friedrich-Wilhelms-Universität und Technischen Hochschule am 23. Juli 1932. Breslau: Trewendt & Granier, 1932. 31 pp.

25. *Arbeitsdienst—Heeresdienst?* Jena: Eugen Diederichs Verlag, 1932. 80 pp.

26. *The Multiformity of Man: Economics of a Mechanized World*. Norwich, Vt.: Beachhead, 1936. 39 pp.
See **32, 38**.

27. *A Classic and a Founder*. Part 1, "The Scientific Grammar of Michael Faraday's Diaries." Part 2, "The Tripartition in the Life of Theophrastus Paracelsus." Contributions to the Philosophy of the Sciences, Dartmouth College, Hanover, N.H., 1937 and 1943. 73 pp.

28. *Out of Revolution: Autobiography of Western Man*. New York: William Morrow & Co., 1938. 735 pp. Reprint eds., London: Jarrolds, 1939; Norwich, Vt.: Argo Books, 1969 (with introduction by Page Smith).
See **22, 35, 45**.

29. *The Artist and His Community*. Commencement exercises at the Stuart School of the Creative Arts, Boston, 1 June 1939. Ann Arbor, Mich.: Edward Brothers, Inc., 1940. 16 pp.

30. *The Christian Future, or, The Modern Mind Outrun*. New York: Charles Scribner's Sons, 1946. 248 pp. Reprint eds., London: S.C.M. Press,

Ltd., 1947 (with foreword by J. H. Oldham and a soliloquy by the author); New York: Harper & Row Publishers, Harper Torchbooks (TB 143), 1966 (with introduction by Harold Stahmer, pp. vii–lv). See 37.

31. *Planetary Man: In Memoriam Oswald Spengler.* Reprinted from *New English Weekly*, 30 May, 6 June, and 13 June 1946. 14 pp.

= 365.

32. *The Multiformity of Man.* Norwich, Vt.: Beachhead, 1949. 71 pp.

= 26 (reprint), chap. 1 added.
See 38.

33. *The Driving Power of Western Civilization: The Christian Revolution of the Middle Ages.* Preface by Karl W. Deutsch. With selected bibliography. Boston: Beacon Press, 1950. 126 pp.

= 28, pp. 453–561.

34. *Der Atem des Geistes.* Frankfurt a.M.: Verlag der Frankfurter Hefte, 1951. 293 pp.

35. *Die europäischen Revolutionen und der Charakter der Nationen.* 2d ed. Stuttgart: W. Kohlhammer Verlag, 1951. 584 pp.

= 22 (revised), 45 (enlarged).
See 28.

36. *Heilkraft und Wahrheit. Konkordanz der politischen und der kosmischen Zeit.* Stuttgart: Evangelisches Verlagswerk GmbH, 1952. 215 pp.

37. *Des Christen Zukunft oder Wir überholen die Moderne.* Revision of the American edition, with the introduction to the English edition by J. H. Oldham, translated into German by Christoph v.d. Bussche und Konrad Thomas. Munich: Kaiser Verlag, 1955. 351 pp. 2d ed., 1956. Paperback ed., Munich and Hamburg: Siebenstern Taschenbuchverlag, 1965, 288 pp., no. 57/58; reprint, Mörs: Brendow Verlag, 1985. See 30.

38. *Der unbezahlbare Mensch.* First 8 chaps. translated from English by Gertie Siemsen. Preface by Walter Dirks. Berlin: Käthe Vogt Verlag, 1955. 201 pp. Paperback ed., Freiburg, Basel, Vienna: Herder Bücherei Bd. 187, 1964. 173 pp.

See 26, 32.

39. *Soziologie.* Bd. 1, *Die Übermacht der Räume.* Stuttgart, Berlin, Cologne, Mainz: W. Kohlhammer, 1956. 335 pp.

= Revised version of 14.

40. *Zurück in das Wagnis der Sprache.* Ein aufzufindender Papyrus. With introduction by Dr. Georg Müller. Berlin: Käthe Vogt Verlag, 1957. 81 pp.

41. *Frankreich—Deutschland. Mythos oder Anrede?* Berlin: Käthe Vogt Verlag, 1957. 106 pp.

42. *Soziologie.* Bd. 2, *Die Vollzahl der Zeiten.* Stuttgart: W. Kohlhammer Verlag GmbH, 1958. 774 pp.

43. *Das Geheimnis der Universität.* Wider den Verfall von Zeitsinn und Sprachkraft. Essays and addresses, 1950–57. Edited and introduced by Dr. Georg Müller, with a contribution by Prof. Dr. Kurt Ballerstedt ("Leben und Werk Eugen Rosenstock-Huessys"). Bibliography of Rosenstock-Huessy's writings compiled by Edward F. Little, B. E. Bergesen, C. Russell Keep, Jr., and Matthias Rang. Stuttgart: W. Kohlhammer Verlag GmbH, 1958. 320 pp.

44. *Bibliography—Biography.* Including a meditation entitled "Biblionomics." Binghamton, N.Y.: Vail Ballou Press, private printing, 1959. 38 pp.
Includes bibliography from **43**.

45. *Die europäischen Revolutionen und der Charakter der Nationen.* Stuttgart: W. Kohlhammer Verlag, 1961. xix + 584 pp.
= Revised version of **35**.
See **28**.

46. *Die Sprache des Menschengeschlechts. Eine leibhaftige Grammatik in vier Teilen.* Bd. 1, Teil 1 und 2. Heidelberg: Verlag Lambert Schneider, 1963. 810 pp.

47. *Die Sprache des Menschengeschlechts. Eine leibhaftige Grammatik in vier Teilen.* Bd. 2, Teil 3 und 4. Heidelberg: Verlag Lambert Schneider, 1964. 904 pp. An index of 26 pp. was printed in page proof but omitted from the published volume.

48. *Dienst auf dem Planeten. Kurzweil und Langeweile im dritten Jahrtausend.* Stuttgart, Berlin, Cologne, Mainz: W. Kohlhammer Verlag GmbH, 1965. 140 pp.
See **64**.

49. *De onbetaalbare mens.* With introduction by Prof. Dr. P. Smits. Vert. H. J. de Koster. Rotterdam: Lemniscaat, 1966. 195 pp.
See **38**.

50. *Ja und Nein.* Autobiographische Fragmente aus Anlass des 80. Ge-

burtstags des Autors im Auftrag der seinen Namen tragenden Gesellschaft. Edited with a postscript by Georg Müller. Heidelberg: Verlag
Lambert Schneider, 1968. 184 pp.

51. *Die Umwandlung.* Die Umwandlung des Wortes Gottes in die Sprache
des Menschengeschlechts. Heidelberg: Verlag Lambert Schneider,
1968. 144 pp.
= **42**, pp. 759–60+; **46**, pp. 119–42+ (and **57**, 1: 111–40); **47**, pp.
759–903.

52. *Judaism despite Christianity.* Edited by Eugen Rosenstock-Huessy. The
letters on Christianity and Judaism between Rosenstock-Huessy and
Franz Rosenzweig, with introduction by Harold Stahmer and essays
"About the Correspondence" by Alexander Altmann and Dorothy
Emmet. University, Ala.: University of Alabama Press, 1969. 198 pp.
Paperback reprint, New York: Schocken Books, 1971.

53. *I Am an Impure Thinker.* With foreword by W. H. Auden. Norwich,
Vt.: Argo Books, 1970. 206 pp.

54. *Speech and Reality.* With introduction by Clinton C. Gardner. Norwich, Vt.: Argo Books, 1970. 201 pp.

AS CO-AUTHOR

55. *Osteuropa und Wir.* Das Problem Russland, erörtert von Dr. Eberhard
Sauer, Dr. Eugen Rosenstock, Prof. Dr. Hans Ehrenberg. "Ostblock
oder Siberien?" by Eugen Rosenstock, pp. 71–78. Schlüchtern: Neu-
werk-Verlag, 1921. 99 pp.

56. *Im Kampf um die Erwachsenenbildung, 1912–1926.* Schriften für Erwachsenenbildung. Im Auftrag der deutschen Schule für Volksforschung und Volksbildung, edited by Dr. Robert von Erdberg. Bd. 1
by Werner Picht and Eugen Rosenstock. Leipzig: Verlag Quelle und
Meyer, 1926. 240 pp.

57. *Das Alter der Kirche. Kapitel und Akten.* With Joseph Wittig. Bd. 1 und
2, 977 pp. Bd. 3, 273 pp. Berlin: Verlag Lambert Schneider, 1927–28.

58. *Das Arbeitslager.* Berichte aus Schlesien von Arbeitern, Bauern, Studenten. With Carl Dietrich von Trotha. Jena: Eugen Diederichs, 1931.
160 pp.

59. *Magna Carta Latina: The Privilege of Singing, Articulating and Reading a*

Language and of Keeping It Alive. With Ford Lewis Battles. Private printing, 1967. 296 pp.

= 63.

AS EDITOR OR CO-EDITOR

60. *Briefe, B.G. und Amalie Niebuhrs an Dore Hensler und an Karsten Niebuhr (1806–1814).* Mitteilungen aus Literaturarchiv in Berlin. Neue Folge 4. Edited by Heinrich Meisner, Erich Schmidt, and Eugen Rosenstock. Berlin: Literaturarchiv-Gesellschaft, 1911. 88 pp.

61. *Theophrast von Hohenheim.* Fünf Bücher über die unsichtbaren Krankheiten. Introduced and edited by Dr. Richard Koch and Prof. Dr. Eugen Rosenstock. Stuttgart: Fr. Fromanns Verlag (H. Kurtz), 1923. 116 pp.

62. *Die Deutsche Schule für Volksforschung und Erwachsenenbildung. Das erste Jahr.* Edited by the Hohenrodter Bund, Theodor Bäuerle, Robert von Erdberg, Wilhelm Flitner, Walter Hofmann, Eugen Rosenstock. Stuttgart: Verlag Silberburg GmbH, 1927. 141 pp.

POSTHUMOUSLY PUBLISHED BOOKS

63. *Magna Carta Latina: The Privilege of Singing, Articulating and Reading a Language and of Keeping It Alive.* With Ford Lewis Battles. Pittsburgh, Pa.: The Pickwick Press, 1975. 296 pp.

= 59.

64. *Planetary Service: A Way into the Third Millennium.* Abridged translation of *Dienst auf dem Planeten,* by Mark Huessy and Freya von Moltke. Norwich, Vt.: Argo Books, 1978. 126 pp.

See 48.

65. *Spraak en Werkelijkheid.* Translation of *Speech and Reality,* by Elias Voet. Haarlem: Vereniging Rosenstock-Huessy-Huis, 1978. viii + 155 pp.

See 53.

66. *The Fruit of Lips, or, Why Four Gospels?* Edited and introduced by Marion Davis Battles. Pittsburgh, Pa.: The Pickwick Press, 1978. 144 pp.

= Original English of 47, pp. 797–903.

See 51, pp. 32–138.

67. *The Origin of Speech.* With introduction by Harold M. Stahmer. Norwich, Vt.: Argo Books, 1981. 141 pp.
= Original English of **47**, pp. 451–594 ("Im Prägstock eines Menschenschlags oder der tägliche Ursprung der Sprache").

68. *Rosenstock-Huessy Papers.* Vol. 1. Norwich, Vt.: Argo Books, 1981. 229 pp.

69. *De Vrucht der Lippen.* Waarom vier evangelien. Translation of *Fruit of Lips* by Elias Voet and Sam Hartman. With introduction by Prof. Dr. J. M. Hasselaar. Baarn: Ten Have, 1981. 126 pp.
See **66**.

ARTICLES

Zeitschrift der Savigny Stiftung für Rechtsgeschichte. Germ. Abt., Weimar.

1913

70. "Neue Literatur über die deutschen Königswahlen." 34 (1913): 487–541. Reviews of: Hermann Bloch, *Die Stauffischen Kaiserwahlen und die Entstehung des Kurfürstentums,* Forschungen, 1911; Johannes Krüger, *Grundsätze und Anschauungen bei den Erhebungen der deutschen Könige in der Zeit von 911 bis 1056,* 1911; Max Buchner, *Die Entstehungsgeschichte der Erzämter und ihre Beziehung zum Werden des Kurkollegs mit Beiträgen zur Entstehungsgeschichte des Pairkollegs in Frankreich,* 1911; Max Buchner, *Die Entstehung und Ausbildung der Kurfürstenfabel,* 1912; Mario Krammer, *Das Kurfürstenkolleg von seinen Anfängen bis zum Zusammenschluss im Renser Kurverein des Jahres 1338,* 1913.

71. "Bruchstücke eines verkürzten Sachsenspiegels." 43 (1913): 408–10.

1916

72. "Die Verdeutschung des Sachsenspiegels." 37 (1916): 498–504.

1929

73. Review (49 [1929]: 509–24) of Karl Heldmann's *Das Kaisertum Karls des Grossen.* Theorien und Wirklichkeit. Quellen zur Verfassungsgeschichte des deutschen Reiches in Mittelalter und Neuzeit, Weimar, 1928.

1930

74. "Erwiderung (auf Dr. Karl Heldmanns Erwiderung S. 625–659)." 51 (1930): 659–67.

Die Hilfe. Gotteshilfe, Selbsthilfe, Staatshilfe, Bruderhilfe. Wochenschrift für Politik, Literatur und Kunst. Edited by Dr. Friedrich Naumann.

1915

75. "Die Verfassung Giolitti." 28 (1915): 448–50.

76. "Heiliges Römisches Reich Deutscher Nation." 48 (1915): 773–74.

1917

77. "Ist der Bundesrat Rat oder Regierung? Zum Streit über Artikel 9 der Reichsverfassung." 51, 20 (December 1917): 735–36.

Hochland. Monatsschrift für alle Gebiete des Wissens, der Literatur und Kunst. Edited by Karl Muth.

1918

78. "Der Kreuzzug des Sternenbanners." Jg. 16 Bd. 1 (November 1918): 113–22.
   Also in 6, pp. 11–20.

79. "Volksstaat und Reich Gottes. Eine Weihnachtsbetrachtung." Jg. 16 Bd. 1 (December 1918): 229–39.
   Also in 6, pp. 21–31.

1919

80. "Die Epochen des Kirchenrechts." Jg. 16 Bd. 2 (April 1919): 64–78.
   Also in 7, pp. 123–49, and 57, pp. 587–617.

81. "Bolschewismus und Christentum." Jg. 16 Bd. 2 (June 1919): 225–28.
   Also in 7, pp. 150–55 (enlarged).

82. "Der Selbstmord Europas." Jg. 16 Bd. 2 (September 1919): 529–53.
   Also in 7, pp. 160–203, and 47, pp. 45–84 (enlarged).

83. "Der Bourgeois." Bearbeitete Anzeige, Dr. Bruno Altmann's "W. Sombart: *Der Bourgeois*. Zur Geistesgeschichte des modernen Wirt-

schaftmenschen" (Berlin, 1914). Jg. 16 Bd. 2 (May 1919): 117–32. See **8**, pp. 251.

1920

84. "Psychotechnik." Jg. 17 (February 1920): 510–26.
= **106**, pp. 37–41 (abbreviated).

85. "Volksbildungstag in Braunau am Inn." Jg. 18 (1920): 237–40.
= **261**.

1923

86. "Das Wesen des Faschismus." Jg. 20 Bd. 2 (1923): 225–34.
Also in **11**, pp. 55–61 (abbreviated).

1931

87. "Das Dritte Reich und die Sturmvögel des Nationalsozialismus," by Ludwig Stahl (pseud.). Jg. 20 Bd. 2 (9 June 1931): 193–211.

1932

88. "Judas Ischariot und die preussischen Konservativen. Zum Auftreten der politischen Diabolik," by Ludwig Stahl (pseud.). Jg. 29 Bd. 2 (April 1932): 1–16.

Die Arbeitsgemeinschaft. Monatsschrift für das gesamte Volks-hochschulwesen. Edited by Werner Picht with Dr. R. von Erdberg and Prof. Dr. A. H. Hollemann, Leipzig.

1920

89. "Der Neubau der deutschen Rechtsgeschichte." (1920): 132–40, 172–81.

1921

90. Review of Alfred Freund's *Technik, ihre Grundlagen für Alle* (Leipzig, n.d. [1920?]). Jg. 2 (1921): 318–19.

91. "Das Dreigestirn der Bildung" (written in 1920). Jg. 2 (1921): 177–99. Also in **56**, pp. 20–42; **413**, pp. 61–87.

1922

92. "Die Akademie der Arbeit in der Universität Frankfurt a.M." Jg. 3 (1922): 147–52.
    = 264, 265.

93. "Die Ausbildung des Volksbildners." Address in Braunau am Inn, 1920. Jg. 3 (1922): 73–90.
    Also in: 56, pp. 150–67; 415, pp. 88–102 (abbreviated).

1923

94. "Angewandte Seelenkunde." On the publication of Karl Haase's *Angewandte Seelenkunde* (Gotha, 1921). Jg. 4 (1923): 129–46.
    Used in 12.

Daimler Werkzeitung. Edited by Dr. Ing. P. Riebensahm und Dr. Eugen Rosenstock, Daimler-Motoren-Gesellschaft. Stuttgart-Untertürkheim, 1919–20.

    1. Jahr

95. "Der Gang des Arbeitstages." 2 (1919): 18–21.

96. "Etwas vom Innenleben fürs Innenleben," by F. Wondratscheck (pseud.). 2 (1919): 24–25.

97. "Leonardo da Vinci." 4 (1919): 45–49.

98. "Italien und Deutschland." 4 (1919): 57–58.

99. "Der Wiederaufbau des Einzelnen." 5 (1919): 81–82.
    = 127.

100. "Gedanken über das Weltgeschehen," by F. Wondratschek (pseud.). 9 (1919): 159.

101. "Neu-Deutschland." Geschichte einer Siedlung. 15/18 (1920): 282–87.

    2. Jahr

102. "Ein Kulturbild aus Norddeutschland." Aus dem alten Prospekt einer Bremer Firma. 1 (1920): 11–13.

103. "Gesunde oder zweckmässige Arbeitshaltung," by Fritz Wurzmann (pseud.). 1 (1920): 14–15.

104. "Die tiefste Quelle der Arbeit," by Kunstgewerbezeichner Friedrich

Wondratschek (pseud.). 1 (1920): 15–16.

105. "Des Kaufmanns Sorgen." Aus den Lebenserinnerungen des Johann Gottlob Nathusius. 1 (1920): 19–24.

106. "Die Leistung der Psychotechnik." 2/4 (1920): 37–41.
     = Abbreviated version of **84**.

107. "Fehlerquellen der praktischen Prüfung." 2/4 (1920): 53.

108. "Sohn und Vater bei der Berufswahl." Aus den Briefen Anselm von Feuerbachs des Älteren. 2/4 (1920): 55–57.

109. "Das Ereignis der Relativitätstheorie." Die Einschaltung der Wissenschaft ins Leben. 5/6 (1920): 63–64.
     Also in **56**, pp. 89–90.

110. "Die Arbeitsgemeinschaft der Astronomen." 5/6 (1920): 73.

111. "Persönliches von Einstein." 5/6 (1920): 73.

112. "Jeder sein eigener Astronom." 5/6 (1920): 84.

113. "Wer hat Recht?" by Meister Fritz Eitel (pseud.). 5/6 (1920): 84–85.

114. "Einleitung zu 'Die Heimkehr' von Hans Heinrich Ehrler." 5/6 (1920): 85.

115. "Arbeitsgemeinschaft." 7 (1920): 87–93.
     = Abbreviated version of **7**, pp. 253–69.

116. "Der Stein der Weisen." Ein altes Gespräch. 8 (1920): 103–5.

Rhein-Mainische Volkszeitung

1924

117. "Die nackte Arbeit." 298 (22 December 1924).
     = **280**.

118. "Arbeiterbildung." 7 November 1924.
     = **281** (with one sentence added).

119. "Des Kaufmanns Dienst am Volke." 193 (6 August 1924): 1–2.

120. "Staatsfamilie oder öffentliches Leben?" 290 (12 August 1924): 1–2.

121. "Die Sprache der Ereignisse." 11 August 1924.
     = **11**, pp. 39–45; **47**, pp. 116–23.

122. "Nachträgliche Erwägungen zur *Angewandte Seelenkunde*. Zusätze zum psychosozialen Programm." 188 (12 August 1924).
= 167, pp. 7–9.

123. "Die wahren Eigenschaften des Politikers." 13 September 1924.
= 11, pp. 46–49; 47, pp. 123–27.

124. "Die Mittel der Politik." 23 September 1924.
= 11, pp. 49–55; 47, pp. 127–34.

1925

125. "Freizeiten her!" 48 (27 February 1925).

1928

126. "Volksbildung in der Universität." 13 August 1928.
= 307.

Frankfurter Zeitung und Handelsblatt

1919

127. "Der Wiederaufbau des Einzelnen." 504 (11 July 1919).
= 99.

1920

128. "Arbeitsrecht und Arbeiterbildung. Die Voraussetzungen der Frankfurter Akademie der Arbeit." Nr. 808 (31 October 1920).
Also in 56, pp. 103–13.

1924

129. "Betriebsverfassung des Hochkapitalismus." Jg. 68 Nr. 125, Erstes Morgenblatt (16 February 1924).

130. "Schulreform und Hochschule." With Dr. Rudolf Ehrenberg. Nr. 662, Abendblatt (4 September 1924): 3–4.

1931

131. "Weil der Geist weht, wo er will . . . Zur Frage Tillichs: Gibt es noch Universität?" Nr. 909 (6 December 1931): 6.

1954

132. "Laodizee—Wie rechtfertigt sich ein Volk?" 14 August 1954.
= Enlarged version of **349**.

Neuwerk. Ein Dienst am Werdenden (Kassel).

1922

133. "Paracelsus in Basel." Jg. 4 (1922): 379–94.
Also in **57**, pp. 729–60, enlarged and improved version ("Der Annus Acceptus des Theophrast von Hohenheim (Paracelsus), Lucas 4: 17–21").

1923–24

134. "Was soll man denn sonst tun?" Jg. 5 (1923–24): 114–19.

135. "ABC in Politik." Jg. 5 (1923–24): 181–89.
Also in **11**, pp. 7–14 (abbreviated).

136. "Deutschlands Kommunisten und Faschisten." Jg. 5 (1923–24): 395–98.

1924

137. "Not und Wende der Arbeiterbewegung." Jg. 4 (1924): 437–43.

1926

138. "Protestantismus und Volksbildung." Jg. 7 (1926): 482–89.
Includes excerpts from **13**.

139. "Die geistigen Bewegungen der Gegenwart." Jg. 8 (1926): 197–205.

Die Kreatur. A quarterly periodical edited by Martin Buber, Joseph Wittig, and Victor von Weizsäcker. Verlag Lambert Schneider, Berlin. Jg. 1, 1926–1927. Jg. 2, 1927–1928. Jg. 3, 1929–1930. Kraus Reprint. Nendeln/Liechtenstein, 1969.

1926–27

140. "Lehrer oder Führer? Zur Polychronie des Menschen." Jg. 1 Heft 1 (1926-27): 52–68.
= **56**, pp. 219–34; **47**, pp. 136–56.

141. "Die Polychronie des Volks." Jg. 1 Heft 4 (1926-27): 409–25.
Also in **47**, pp. 156–75 ("Die Polyphonie des Volks").

1927–28

142. "Kirche und Arbeit—Eine Rede." Jg. 2 (1927-1928): 158–80.

1929–1930

143. "Die Gefangenschaft des Volkes." Jg. 3 (1929-30): 61–68.
Also in **20**, pp. 9–15.

144. "Die rückwärts gelebte Zeit." Unsere Erfahrungen von 1918 bis 1928. Jg. 3 (1929-30): 101–17.
Also in **47**, pp. 178–97.

Una Sancta. Ein Ruf an die Christenheit. Quarterly edited by Alfred von Martin.

1927

145. "Augustinus und Thomas in ihrer Bedeutung für das Denken unserer Zeit." Jg. 3 Heft 1 (1927): 14–22.
Also in **57**, pp. 655–73, enlarged ("Augustin und Thomas in ihrer Wirhung auf unser Denken").

146. "Alphons Maria Ratisbonne, ein neuer Bruder im Herrn, von Theodor de Bussieres." Mit einer Einleitung über Nationalsozialismus und Antisemitismus von P. Alois Mager O.pp.B. (Munich and Rome, 1926). Jg. 3 (1927): 490–91.

147. Review of Nikolaus Berdjajew's *Das neue Mittelalter. Betrachtungen über das Schicksal Russlands und Europas* (Darmstadt, 1927). Die Ostkirche Sonderheft der Vierteljahresschrift *Una Sancta*. Edited by Nicolas von Arseniew und Alfred von Martin. 1927, pp. 125–28.

Zeitwende, Kultur, Theologie, Politik

1928

148. "Leben und Arbeit." Jg. 4 Erste Hälfte (January–June 1928): 341–53. Elaboration of an address at the ecclesiastical-social congress in Düsseldorf.
Also in **20**, pp. 42–55.

1929

149. "Die Schranke des Sozialpolitikers." Jg. 5 (1929): 97–107. Also appeared as a reprint.

150. "Der Sozialismus als Antithese." Jg. 5 (1929): 193–203.

1930

151. "Menschenmacht und Massenmacht." Jg. 6 (January–June 1930): 77–81. Also appeared as a reprint.

Frankfurter Hefte. Zeitschrift für Kultur und Politik. Edited by Eugen Kogon assisted by Walter Dirks.

1948

152. "Symblysma oder Überschwang der Jesuiten." Jg. 3 Heft 11 (November 1948): 1023–32.
    Also in **34,** pp. 239–73 (enlarged).

1951

153. "Die jüdischen Antisemiten oder die akademische Form der Judenfrage." Jg. 6 Heft 1 (1951): 8–17.
    Also in **43,** pp. 44–55.

154. "Der dritte Weltkrieg." Jg. 6 Heft 1 (1951): 796–800.
    Also in **45,** pp. 517–22.

1959

155. "Die Bemannung der Hochschule." Jg. 14 Heft 1 (January 1959): 55–66.
    = Abbreviated version of **42,** pp. 683–709.

156. "An die Russen. Naturforschung oder Gesellschaftslehre?" Jg. 14 Heft 2 (1959): 97–102.
    = **415,** pp. 3–6.

157. "Die Fortschritte der Gesellschaft und die Soziologie. Universität oder Schule?" Jg. 14 Heft 3 (1959): 183–92.
    = **415,** pp. 6–11.

Neues Abendland. Zeitschrift für Politik, Kultur und Geschichte.

1953

158. "Ich bin ein unreiner Denker. Vom Töchterlich-Werden des Denkens." Jg. 8 Heft 1 (1953): 11–24.
    Also in 28, pp. 740–50 ("Farewell to Descartes"); 43, pp. 97–112; 53, pp. 1–19 ("Farewell to Descartes").

159. "Partner und Stämme der Industrie. Der Marxismus hat seine Zugkraft als Heilswahn eingebüsst." Jg. 8 Heft 1 (1953): 323–37.

160. "Was ist der Mensch? Eine Laienabwehr." Jg. 8 (1953): 707–18.
    Also in 43, pp. 134–45.

1954

161. "Dich und mich. Lehre oder Mode?" Jg. 9 Heft 11 (November 1954): 643–52.
    Also in 43, pp. 149–59.

162. "Dich und Ich. Was folgt aus der empirischen Grammatik?" Jg. 9 Heft 12 (December 1954): 719–27.
    Also in 43, pp. 160–68.

Offene Welt. Zeitschrift für Wirtschaft, Politik und Gesellschaft.

1958

163. "Bestimmung der Wirtschaft in einer revolutionierten Welt." Nr. 57 (October 1958): 447–58.

1959

164. "Friedensbedingungen einer Weltwirtschaft." Nr. 59 (January–February 1959): 34–48, 60.

1963

165. "Europas Amerika und Amerikas Europa." Nr. 79 (1963): 108–13.
    Also in 47, pp. 310–19.

Mitteilungen der Eugen Rosenstock-Huessy-Gesellschaft. Folge 1–28, 1963–79. After 1980, *Mitteilungsblatt der Eugen Rosenstock-Huessy-Gesellschaft.*

1968

166. "Tribute from a 'Post-Goethian.'" Folge 8 (June 1968): 3. Originally a Dartmouth College paper (1949).

1969

167. "Nachträgliche Erwägungen Eugen Rosenstock-Huessys zur *Angewandten Seelenkunde* aus dem Erscheinungsjahr 1924."
1. "Zusätze zum psychosozialen Programm." *Rhein-Mainische Volkszeitung* 188 (12 August 1924).
= 122.
2. "Brief an Joachim Sindermann vom Dezember 1924." *Mitteilungen der Eugen Rosenstock-Huessy-Gesellschaft* Folge 10 (June 1969): 7–11.

168. "Anfänge meines Friedensdienstes." Folge 11 (December 1969): 2.

169. "Prolog (und Epilog) zu den Briefen Eugen Rosenstocks und Franz Rosenzweigs—fünfzig Jahre später übersetzt aus *Judaism despite Christianity*. Folge 11 (December 1969): 9–12.
= Translation of 52, pp. 71–76.

1970

170. "Invocatio vom 28.6.1970." Folge 13 (November 1970): 1–2.

1975

171. "Die weggelaufene Eschatologie." Folge 22 (November 1975): 1–2.
= 694.

1976

172. "Zur Problematik des religiösen Sozialismus. Über Tillichs *Masse und Geist.*" Folge 23 (April 1976): 1–6. Manuscript, 1922.

1977

173. "Die Mitschöpfer, eine Einführung in die Universalgeschichte." Folge 25 (April 1977): 1–4. A very poor and faulty translation of "The Co-Creators," a draft of the preface to both volumes of *Soziologie*. The four-page manuscript is in the archive of the Eugen Rosenstock-Huessy-Gesellschaft in Bethel-Bielefeld.

174. "Zwei oder Drei in meinem Namen." Folge 26 (October 1977): 1–3. Thoughts of Rosenstock-Huessy, selected by Franz Utt.

175. "Einladung zur Zeitbuchreihe 'Epoche.'" Folge 25 (April 1977): 4–6.

1981

176. "Akademik oder Argonautik." 1981, pp. 5–10.
     = Enlarged version of 377.

1982

177. "Aphorismen über den Aphorismus." 1982, pp. 17–20.
     = 327.

1983

178. "Künftige Widersacher der Kirche." 1983, pp. 2–10.
     = 401.

1984

179. "Das Gehirn kann nicht bereuen." 1984, pp. 2–9. Excerpts from an interview with Hans Fischer-Barnicol in Heidelberg, used in a radio broadcast on 10 October 1964.

1985

180. "Was kostet die Geschichte?" 1985, pp. 2–5.
     = 46, pp. 348–349 (Das Auf beim Hören und das Los beim Sagen).

181. "Das Gespräch vor Zeugen." 1985, pp. 5–9. Written in 1919.
     = 258.

The American People's Encyclopedia. New York: Grolier, Inc., 1962.

182. "Abelard, Pierre." 1: 22–23. Unsigned.

183. "Animism." 2: 46. Unsigned.

184. "Aristotle." 2: 399–400. Unsigned.

185. "Augustine, Saint." 2: 776–77. Unsigned.

186. "Bacon, Roger." 2: 919–20. Unsigned.

187. "Conceptualism." 5: 1022–23. Unsigned.

188. "Concordance." 6: 5–6. Unsigned.

189. "Confessions of Saint Augustine." 6: 35–36. Unsigned.

190. "Cross." 6: 556–59. Unsigned.

191. "Dante, Alighieri." 6: 775–80.

192. "David." 6: 806–7. Unsigned.

193. "Descartes, René." 6: 1000–1003.

194. "Dialectic." 7: 47–48.

195. "Dialogue." 7: 48–49.

196. "Dionysius the Areopagite." 7: 122–23. Unsigned.

197. "Divine Comedy, The." 7: 176–78.

198. "Duns Scotus." 7: 410.

199. "Edwards, Jonathan." 7: 615–17.

200. "Emerson, Ralph Waldo." 7: 859–61.

201. "Existentialism." 8: 201–4. Unsigned.

202. "Grimm's Law." 9: 1015. Unsigned.

203. "Name." 13: 1064–68. Unsigned.

204. "Newman, John Henry Cardinal." 14: 304–6. Unsigned.

205. "Paracelsus." 15: 26–27. Unsigned.

206. "Plato." 15: 650–57. Unsigned.

207. "Republic." 16: 429–30. Unsigned.

208. "Republic." 16: 430–31. Unsigned.

209. "Saint-Simon, Claude Henri de." 16: 914–15. Unsigned.

210. "Socrates." Plato, Socrates, and Athens. 17: 546–47. Unsigned.

211. "Timaeus." 18: 546–48. Unsigned.

212. "University." 19: 68–69. Unsigned.

213. "Vahlen, Johannes." 19: 144.

214. "Vaihinger, Hans." 19: 144–45.

215. "Valentinius." 19: 152–53.

216. "Vampire." 19: 164.

217. "Ventris, Michael George Francis." 19: 239–41.

218. "Venus." 19: 245–46.

219. "Verner, Karl Adolph." 19: 272.

220. "Vico, Giovanni Battista." 19: 301–2.

221. "Walton, Izaak." 19: 460.

222. "Webb, Beatrice." 19: 590.

223. "Webb, Sidney James, 1st Baron Passfield." 19: 591.

224. "Weber, Max." 19: 592–93.

225. "Webster, Daniel." 19: 593–96.

226. "Weizsäcker, Freiherr Viktor von." 19: 613–14.

227. "Wesley, John." 19: 633–35.

228. "Whitehead, Alfred North." 19: 703–5.

229. "Whitman, Walt." 19: 712–16.

230. "Wieland, Christopher Martin." 19: 724.

231. "William Ockman." 19: 746–48.

232. "William of Champeaux." 19: 748.

233. "Winckelmann, Johann Joachim." 19: 771–72.

234. "Wittig, Joseph." 19: 810–11.

235. "Wolf, Friedrich August." 19: 812–13.

236. "Wolfram von Eschenbach." 19: 816.

237. "Wundt, Wilhelm Max." 19: 934–35.

238. "Wycliffe, John." 19: 938–39.

239. "X." 19: 955.

240. "Xenophon." 19: 957–58.

241. "Y." 19: 967.

242. "Z." 19: 1029.

243. "Zarathustra." 19: 1038–39.

244. "Zen." 19: 1042–43.

245. "Zeno of Citium." 19: 1044–45.

246. "Zeno of Elea." 19: 1045–46.

247. "Zeus." 19: 1048–50.

248. "Zoroastrism." 19: 1079–82.

249. "Zweig, Stephan." 19: 1086–87. Unsigned.

250. "Zwingli, Huldreich." 19: 1087–88.

251. "Zur Ausbildung des mittelalterlichen Festkalenders." *Archiv für Kulturgeschichte*, Leipzig and Berlin. Bd. 10 (1912): 272–82.

252. "Die Zuverlässigkeit der 'Lebensnachrichten über B. G. Niebuhr.'" *Historische Zeitschrift*, Munich and Berlin. Bd. 110 Folge 3 Bd. 14 (1913): 566–73.

253. "Würzburg, das erste geistliche Herzogtum in Deutschland." *Historische Vierteljahresschrift*, Leipzig. Jg. 24 der ganzen Reihe, Jg. 16 (1913): 68–77.

254. "Synodalis." *Neues Archiv. Gesellschaft für ältere deutsche Geschichtskunde*, Hannover and Leipzig. Bd. 38 (1913): 307–9.

255. "Principium Doctoris." *Festgabe für Rudolf Sohm zum goldenen Doktorjubiläum*, pp. 87–101. Munich and Leipzig: Duncker und Humbolt, 1914.

256. Review of Edwin Mayer-Homberg's *Die fränkischen Volksrechte im Mittelalter*, Bd. 1, *Die fränkischen Volksrechte und das Reichsrecht* (Weimar, 1912). *Historische Zeitschrift*, Munich and Berlin. 113. Bd. der ganzen Reihe, Folge 3 Bd. 17 (1914): 340–45.

257. "Der Grund der inneren Krise." *Das Neue Deutschland* Jg. 6 (November 1917): 87–89.

258. "Gespräch vor Zeugen." Verlagsdruckerei Würzburg, 1919. Archiv der Eugen Rosenstock-Huessy-Gesellschaft. 4 pp.
= **181**.

259. "Der ewige Prozess des Rechts gegen den Staat." *Zeitschrift für Rechtsphilosophie in Lehre und Praxis* Jg. 2 (1919): 219–41. Also appeared as a reprint.
Also in **46**, pp. 578–602 ("Der Sprachprozess gegen den Staat. Aus den letzten Monaten des Kaiserreichs").

260. "Abschlag" and "Abschlagen." *Deutsches Rechtswörterbuch, Wörterbuch der älteren deutschen Rechtssprache*, 1: 252–60. Edited by Richard Schröder und Eberhard Freiherr von Künssberg. Weimar: Hermann Böhlaus Nachfolger, 1914–32.

261. "Volksbildungstag in Braunau a.I." *Donauland*. Monatsschrift für

alle Gebiete des Wissens, der Literatur und Kunst, Kempten. Jg. 4
Bd. 2 (1921): 237–40.
= 85.

262. "Die Unterrichtsmethode der Akademie der Arbeit in Frankfurt
a.m." *Zentralblatt für die gesamte Unterrichtsverwaltung in Preussen*
Jg. 63 Nr. 397 (1921): 302–4.
= 263, 276.
Also in 56, pp. 122–28.

263. "Die Unterrichtsmethode der Akademie der Arbeit in Frankfurt
a.m." *Zentralblatt der christlichen Gewerkschaften Deutschlands* Jg. 21
Nr. 10 (1921): 244–46.
= 262, 276.
Also in 56, pp. 122–28.

264. "Die Akademie der Arbeit in der Universität Frankfurt a.m." *Der
Grundstein* 43 (1921): 288–89.
= 92, 265.

265. "Die Akademie der Arbeit in der Universität Frankfurt a.m." *Freiheit*
(Graz), November 1921.
= 92, 264.

266. "Partei und Volksbildung." Jubiläums-Nummer der *Frankfurter
Volkszeitung*. Blatt 3 Nr. 226 (1 October 1921): 17.
Also in 56, pp. 160–75.

267. "Zwölf Bücher." *Die Zwölf Wegbereiter*, pp. 43–45. Ein Almanach
persönlicher Beratung für das Jahr 1921. Edited by Leo Weismantel.
Munich and Frankfurt: Verlag der Arbeitsgemeinschaft, 1921.

268. Review of Dipl.,-Ing. Dr. E. W. Seyfert's *Der Arbeiternachwuchs in der
deutschen Maschinenindustrie* (Berlin, 1920). *Werkstattstechnik* Heft 3
(1921): 76–77.

269. "Laienbildung oder Volksbildung?" *Volksbildungsarchiv* Bd. 8 Heft
12 (1921): 381–88.

270. "Kastengeist und Mandarinentum." *Beamtenjahrbuch*, April 1922, pp.
166–68.

271. "Die philosophischen Grundlagen des Arbeitsrechts." *Juristische
Wochenschrift* Jg. 51 Heft 8 (15 April 1922): 560–62.

272. "An die Mitarbeiter der Akademie der Arbeit." Frankfurt a.M.:
Werner und Winter GmbH, 13 March 1922. Archiv der Eugen Ro-

senstock-Huessy-Gesellschaft. 4 pp.

273. "Die Welt vor dem Blick der Kirche." *Die Tat.* Monatsschrift für die Zukunft deutscher Kultur. Jg. 15 (1923): 8–20.
= 274.
Also in 57, pp. 761–84.

274. "Die Welt vor dem Blick der Kirche." *Kirche und Wirklichkeit,* pp. 226–40. Ein katholisches Zeitbuch, edited by Ernst Michel. Jena: Eugen Diederichs, 1923.
= 273.
Also in 57, pp. 761–84.

275. "Das Herz der Welt. Ein Massstab der Politik." *Kirche und Wirklichkeit,* pp. 241–65. Edited by Ernst Michel. Jena: Eugen Diederichs, 1923.
Also in 57, pp. 3–44.

276. "Die Unterrichtsmethode der Akademie der Arbeit in Frankfurt a.M." *G.A.D.* (*Gewerkschaft der Angestellten*), Jablonec, Czechoslovakia. Jg. 1 (1923).
= 262, 263.
Also in 56, pp. 122–28.

277. Review of Ferdinand Ossendowski's *Tiere, Menschen und Götter* (translation of the original American edition). *Literarische Beilage der Augsburger Postzeitung* 15 (9 April 1924): 59.

278. Review of Otto Selz's *Die Gesetze der produktiven und reproduktiven Geistestätigkeiten* (Bonn, 1924). *Archiv für Erwachsenenbildung.* Organ des Hohenrodter Bundes. Jg. 1 (1924): 178.

279. "Unternehmer und Volksordnung." *Der Neue Merkur* Jg. 7 (1924): 997–1004.
Also in 56, pp. 176–82.

280. "Die nackte Arbeit." *Literarische Beilage der Augsburger Postzeitung* 44 (29 October 1924): 1.
= 117.

281. "Arbeiterbildung." *Blätter der Volkshochschule Breslau* Jg. 3 Nr. 35 (July–September 1924): 13–17.
= 118.

282. "Andragogik." *Archiv für Erwachsenenbildung.* Organ des Hohenrodter Bundes. Jg. 1 (1924): 248–76.

Also in 56, pp. 193–219.

283. "Hegel und unser Geschlecht." *Der Neue Merkur* Jg. 8 (1924–25): 360–62.

284. "Sozialpolitik und Arbeitsrecht." *Arbeitskunde*, pp. 64–84. Grundlagen, Bedingungen und Ziele der wirtschaftlichen Arbeit, edited by Johannes Riedel. Leipzig and Berlin: Druck und Verlag B.G. Teubner, 1925.

285. "Das Versiegen der Wissenschaft und der Ursprung der Sprache." *Der Neue Merkur* Jg. 8 Nr. 10 (July 1925): 814–37.

Also in 46, pp. 655–83.

286. "Werkstatthygiene." *Die Räder* Jg. 6 Nr. 12 (1925): 139–40.

287. "Werkstattkommandite." *Reichsarbeitsblatt* (Nichtamtl. Teil) Nr. 38 (1925): 615–18.

288. "Die seelischen Wirkungen der modernen Arbeitsordnung." *Berufsschule und Leben*, pp. 26–31. Frankfurt, 1925. Elaboration of two lectures given on 9 and 10 December 1925, at the Berufsschulwoche, Frankfurt a.M.

289. "Der Ingenieur im Kampf gegen die Unrentabilität des Betriebes." *Hessische Hochschulzeitung* Jg. 15 Heft 4 (1926): 42–45.

Also in 56, pp. 186–93.

290. "Macht und Schranken der Industrialisierung des Reichs." *Der Arbeitgeber.* Zeitschrift der Vereinigung der Deutschen Arbeitgeberverbände. Jg. 16 Nr. 7, Berlin (1 April 1926): 129–34. A lecture at the meeting of the Vereinigung der Deutschen Arbeitgeber-Verbände, 12 March 1926.

= 291.

Also in 20, 16–31.

291. "Macht und Schranken der Industrialisierung des Reichs." *Hessische Hochschulzeitung.* Amtliches Organ der Studentenschaft der Technischen Hochschule Darmstadt. Amtliches Mitteilungsblatt der Kreisleitung des Kreises VI der Deutschen Studentenschaft. Jg. 15 Heft 9 and 10 (7 and 20 July 1926): 101–4, 113–15.

= 290.

Also in 20, pp. 16–31.

292. "Der Begriff des Lebensraumes und die Methode der Soziologie." *Die Schildgenossen.* Zeitschrift für die katholische Laienbewegung. Jg. 6, Würzburg (1926): 233–46.

From **8**, pp. 1–16.

293. "Robert von Erdberg, 6. Juni 1866–6. Juni 1926." *Unterhaltungsbeilage der Schlesischen Zeitung* Nr. 45 (6 June 1926): 1.

294. "Gesetz oder Sakrament? Zur Ehediskussion." *Eckart. Blätter für evangelische Geisteskultur* Jg. 3, Berlin (1927): 249–51.
= Revised version of **57**, pp. 927–36 ("Die Ehe—Gesetz oder Sakrament?").

295. "Vom Neuland zwischen Pädagogik und Demagogik." *Der Kunstwart* Jg. 40 (1926–27): 357–65.

296. "Die Verarmung des Typs. Gemeinsamkeiten und Gegensätze der Wesensart." *Der Weisse Ritter* 7 (1927): 142–45.
= **297.**
See **313.**

297. "Die Verarmung des Typs. Gemeinsamkeiten und Gegensätze der Wesensart." *Ein neuer Weg*, pp. 46–49. Potsdam: L. Voggenreiter, 1927.
= **296.**
See **313.**

298. "Notiz über sich selbst." *Ein neuer Weg*, pp. 141–42. Potsdam: L. Voggenreiter, 1927.

299. "Die geistige Struktur des deutschen Ostens." *Abendland. Deutsche Monatshefte für europäische Kultur, Politik und Wissenschaft.* Heft 3 (1927): 75–78.

300. "Universität und Technische Hochschule." *Breslauer Hochschul-Rundschau* Jg. 18 Nr. 1 (January 1927): 1–3.
= **319** ("Die Freizeit des Akademikers"—revised).

301. "Hochschule und Arbeitslager." *Die gelbe Zeitung.* Bericht und Botschaft der Bündischen Jugend Deutschlands. Heft 5–6 (Christmas 1927): 81–84.
= **302, 310.**

302. "Hochschule und Arbeitslager." *Schlesische Hochschulblätter.* Amtliches Mitteilungsblatt. Nr. 2 (June 1927): 17–19.
= **301, 310.**

303. "Religionsphilosophie der Gesellschaft." *Jahresberichte der schlesischen Gesellschaft für vaterländische Kultur* Jg. 100 (1927): 106–8.

304. "Idealistisches und namentliches Denken." *Archiv für Rechtsphilo-*

sophie Bd. 21 (1927–28): 272–74.

= 305.

305. "Idealistisches und namentliches Denken." *Archiv für Rechts- und Wirtschaftsphilosophie* Bd. 21 (1927–28): 420–22.

= 304 (enlarged).

306. "Leben und Arbeit." *Eine Aussprache zwischen evangelischen Männern und Frauen auf dem 25. kirchlich-sozialen Kongress in Düsseldorf 1927*, pp. 36–47. Leipzig and Erlangen: A. Deichert, 1928.

307. "Volksbildung in der Universität." *Blätter der Volkshochschule Breslau* Jg. 8 (1928): 162–66.

= 126.

308. "Das Arbeitslager für Jungarbeiter, Jungbauern und Jungakademiker in Löwenberg vom 14.–31. März 1928." *Freie Volksbildung, Neue Folge des Archivs für Erwachsenenbildung*, Jg. 3 (1928): 217–24.

309. "Hochschule und Arbeitslager." *Mitteilungen des Verbandes der deutschen Hochschulen* 8 (1928): 101–5.

310. "Hochschule und Arbeitslager. Zum Arbeitslager der ostelbischen Freischaren Ostern 1927." *Die Volksgruppe.* Beiträge zum schlesischen Volksbildungswerk. Heft 1 (1928): 6–7.

= 301, 302.

311. "Die Namen Deutsch und Völkisch." *Die Schildgenossen* Jg. 8 (1928): 536–43.

312. "Symbol und Sitte als Lebensmacht." *Zeitschrift für evangelische Pädagogik* Jg. 3 Heft 4 (1928): 145–55. A lecture delivered at the fifth Religious Pedagogy Conference in Magdeburg, 11 April 1928. Abbreviated and garbled stenograph.

See 323.

313. "The Impoverishment of the Type." *Britain and Germany*, pp. 111–20. Edited by Rolf Gardiner and Heinz Rocholl. London: William and Norgate, Ltd., 1928.

See 296, 297.

314. "Ein Wort von Augustin und eins von Goethe." *Aus unbekannten Schriften*, pp. 53–57. Festgabe für Martin Buber zum 50. Geburtstag. Berlin: Verlag Lambert Schneider, 1928.

315. "Unser Volksname Deutsch und die Aufhebung des Herzogtums Bayern." *Mitteilungen der Schlesischen Gesellschaft für Volkskunde* 29

(1929): 1–66.

= **18**.

316. "Dienstpflicht?" *Deutsche Rundschau* 119 (April–May–June 1929): 1–15.

317. "Erwachsenenbildung und schlesisches Arbeitslager." *Schlesische Monatshefte* 2 (1929): 112–17.

318. "Jugend und Alter in der modernen Gesellschaft." *Kölner Blätter für Berufserziehung* Jg. 5 (1929): 147–61.

319. "Die Freizeit des Akademikers." *Freizeitgestaltung, Grundsätze und Erfahrungen zur Erziehung berufsgebundener Menschen,* pp. 17–26. Edited by Fritz Klatt. Stuttgart, 1929.

    = **300** (revised).

320. Interview. *Freizeitgestaltung,* pp. 154–56. Edited by Fritz Klatt. Stuttgart, 1929.

321. "Kirche und Beruf." *Soziale Praxis* Jg. 38 (1929): 468–70.

322. "Vom Staat zum Stamm." *Der Kunstwart* Jg. 42 (1929): 377–82.

323. "Symbol und Sitte als Lebenmächte." *Die Erziehung.* Monatsschrift für den Zusammenhang von Kultur und Erziehung in Wissenschaft und Leben. Jg. 4 (1929): 341–61.

    See **312**.

324. "Die ungeschriebene Verfassung." *Akademische Rundschau,* Technische Hochschule, Breslau. Jg. 1 Nr. 2 (July 1929): 3–12.

    = **18**.

    Also in **20**, pp. 32–41.

325. "A maganjog nehany uj alapfogalmarol." *Kereskedelmi Jog, Hiteljogi Es Gazdasagpolitikai Folyoirat,* Budapest. 1 November, 1 December 1929, pp. 245–47, 269–71.

    = **338**.

326. "Protestantismus und Seelenführung." *Protestantismus als Kritik und Gestaltung,* pp. 224–28. Edited by Paul Tillich. Zweites Buch des Kairos-Kreises. Darmstadt: Otto Reichl Verlag, 1929.

    Parts reprinted in **431**, pp. 224–28, 248–53.

327. "Aphorismus und Kurztitel." *Eckart. Blätter für evangelische Geisteskultur* Jg. 5 Berlin (1929): 197–99.

    = **177**.

328. "Die Arbeitslager innerhalb der Erwachsenenbildung." *Jahrbuch der Erwachsensenenbildung* 2 (1930): 28–47.

= 21.

329. "Erwachsenenbildung und Betriebspolitik." *Sozialrechtliches Jahrbuch* 1 (1930): 135–50.

330. "Über 'Reich,' 'Staat' und 'Stadt' in Deutschland von 1230–1235." *Mitteilungen des österreichischen Instituts für Geschichtsforschung* Bd. 44 (1930): 401–16. Comments on Emil Franzel's *König Heinrich VII von Hohenstaufen. Studium zur Geschichte des Staats in Deutschland* (Prague, 1929).

331. "Die Kirche am Ende der Welt." In *Credo Ecclesiam*, pp. 161–75. Festgabe zum 70. Geburtstag D. Wilhelm Zöllners. Im Auftrage des Kampfbundes christlicher Arbeiter und in Verbindung mit Johannes Müller-Schwefe, herausgegeben von Hans Ehrenberg. Gütersloh: C. von Bertelsmann, 1930.

Also in 46, pp. 205–20 ("Die Lust am Lästern").

332. "Reverendissime!" Widmungsblatt, *Credo Ecclesiam* (1930).

See 331.

333. "Die Kirche und die Völker." Abriss und Überblick. *Credo Ecclesiam* (1930), pp. 285–95.

See 331.

334. "Deutsche Nation und deutsche Universität." Zur intensiven Seite der Hochschulreform. *Deutsche Rundschau* 225 (October–November–December 1930): 215–25.

335. "The Social Function of Adult Education." *Bulletin of the World Association for Adult Education*, London. 44 (1930): 10–16.

336. "Revolution als politischer Begriff in der Neuzeit." *Abhandlungen der schlesischen Gesellschaft für vaterländische Kultur*, pp. 83–124. Geistes-wissenschaftliche Reihe 5. Heft, Festgabe der Rechts- und Staatswissenschaftlichen Fakultät in Breslau für Paul Heilborn zum 70. Geburtstag, 6. Februar 1931. Breslau: M. & H. Marcus, 1931.

= 23.

337. "Sklaverei oder Regeneration?" Gedanken zur Gefährdung des Arbeitsdienstes *Hannoversche Landeszeitung. Deutsche Volkszeitung. Niedersächsische Zeitung. Neue Hannoversche Zeitung* Jg. 65 Nr. 54 (21 June 1932): 1; and Nr. 55 (22 June 1932): 1.

338. "Über einige neue Grundbegriffe des Privatrechts." Nach einem

Vortrag gehalten in der Peter Patmany-Universität in Budapest am
2. Oktober 1929. *Beiträge zum Wirtschaftsrecht*, pp. 213–28. Edited by
F. Klausing, H. C. Nipperdey, A. Nussbaum. Bd. 1, Festschrift für E.
Heymann. Marburg in Hessen: N. G. Elwertsche Verlagsbuchhand-
lung, G. Braun, 1931.

= 325.

339. "Grundsätze über eine Bildungsstätte für erwachsene Arbeiter."
Denkschrift, September 1920. *Die Akademie der Arbeit an der Univer-
sität Frankfurt a.M., 1921–1931. Zu ihrem zehnjährigen Bestehen im
Auftrag des Dozenten-Kollegiums*, pp. 31–37. Edited by Ernst Michel.
Frankfurt a.M., 1931.

Also in 56, pp. 92–98.

340. "Die Stellung der Akademie unter den übrigen Schulen." Aus einem
Brief des ersten Leiters. *Die Akademie der Arbeit in der Universität
Frankfurt a.M.*, pp. 42–44. Frankfurt a.M., 1931.

Also in 56, pp. 115–18.

341. "Sozialer Dienst der Universität und ihrer Studenten." *I.S.S. Annals,
Annales universitaires, Annalen des Weltstudentenwerkes*, Geneva. Heft
3 (1932): 46–48.

= Abbreviated translation of 342, 343.

342. "Student and University Service to the Community." *I.S.S. Annals,
Annales universitaires, Annalen des Weltstudentenwerkes* Heft 3 (1932):
4–10.

= 341, 343.

343. "Les Étudiants et l'université au service de la société. Rôle social de
l'université." *I.S.S. Annals, Annales universitaires, Annalen des Welt
studentenwerkes* Heft 3 (1932): 60–63.

= 341, 342.

344. "Die Judenemanzipation." *Bayerische Israelitische Gemeindezeitung* 8
Nr. 1 (1932): 3–6.

From 22, pp. 372–77.

345. "Der Arbeitsdienst als Erzieher." *Die Jugendpflege*. Zentrale Monatsschrift für Jugendpflege, Jugendbewegung und Leibesübungen. Jg.
9 (1932): 177–81.

346. "Zur Strategie des Arbeistdienstes." *Freie Volksbildung* Jg. 7 (1932):
275–84.

347. "Das Volk zwischen Himmel und Erde." *Das evangelische Deutsch-

land. Kirchliche Rundschau. Jg. 9 (1932): 219–20.

From **25**, pp. 37–46 ("Die religiös-philosophische Dialektik. Das Volk zwischen Himmel und Erde").

348. "Henrich Steffens." *Schlesische Lebensbilder* Bd. 4, Breslau (1932): 264–80.

349. "Die Geschichtsnot und die Gefahr der Barbarei." *Gartenlaube,* pp. 831–33. Illustriertes Familienblatt (Rubrik: Wissenschaft an der Wende). Leipzig, 1932.

= **132**, enlarged ("Laodizee—Wie rechtfertigt sich ein Volk?").

350. "Weshalb heissen wir Deutsche?" *Kölnische Zeitung* 468 (27 August 1932). Unterhaltungsblatt.

351. "Mannwerdung. Zur Initiative des Reiches in der 'Jugendertüchtigung.'" *Die Erziehung,* November 1932, pp. 102–18.

352. "Arbeitslager." *Handwörterbuch des deutschen Volksbildungswesens,* columns 138–45. Edited by Heinrich Becker, Georg Adolf Narciss, Rudolf Mirbt. Breslau, 1933.

353. "The Army Enlisted against Nature." *Journal of Adult Education,* 1934, pp. 271–74. Formerly *Journal of the American Association for Adult Education.*

354. "The Predicament of History." *Journal of Philosophy* 32, no. 4 (14 February 1935): 93–100.

355. Reviews of Crane Brinton's *The Anatomy of Revolution* (New York, 1938) and Roger Bigelow Merriman's *Six Contemporaneous Revolutions* (New York, 1938). *American Historical Review* 24 (July 1939): 882–84.

356. "Youth and Authority." *American Youth: An Enforced Reconnaissance,* pp. 3–25. Edited by Thatcher Winslow and Frank P. Davidson. Cambridge: Harvard University Press, 1940.

357. "A Peace Within." *American Youth: An Enforced Reconnaissance,* pp. 197–206. Edited by Thatcher Winslow and Frank P. Davidson. Cambridge: Harvard University Press, 1940.

= Translation of **56**, pp. 3–9 ("Ein Landfrieden. Eine Denkschrift von 1912").

358. "Correction on Paying the Price." Letter to *The Dartmouth,* 23 February 1940, pp. 2–3.

359. "Rendering Accounts." In three parts. *The Dartmouth,* 5 March 1940,

pp. 1, 3; 6 March 1940, pp. 1, 3; 7 March 1940, pp. 1, 3.

360. "What They Should Make Us Think" and "What We Should Make Them Do." Two addresses given 21 May and 23 May 1940, respectively. *Annual Conference of CCC Educational Advisers*, pp. 35–43. First Corps area. Dartmouth College, Hanover, N.H.

361. "A Balance Sheet." Confidential report on Camp William James, 15 February 1941. Argo Books archive, Norwich, Vt. 30 pp.

362. Letter to *The Christian Newsletter*, edited by J. H. Oldham. 101 (1 October 1941): 3–4.

363. "The Domestic Parallel to War." As told to George F. Havell. *Free America*, January 1942, pp. 14–15.

364. "Hitler and Israel, or, On Prayer." *Journal of Religion* 25, no. 2 (April 1945): 129–39.
    Also in 52, pp. 178–94.

365. "Planetary Man." In memoriam Oswald Spengler. *New English Weekly*, 30 May 1946, pp. 68–69; 6 June 1946, pp. 77–78; 13 June 1946, pp. 88–89.
    = 31.

366. "Ascent of Taurus." With E. F. Little. *Canadian Alpine Journal*, Chicago. 30 (1947): 15–28.

367. "Rückblick auf die 'Kreatur.'" *Deutsche Beiträge zur Geistigen Überlieferung*, 1: 208–16. Chicago: University of Chicago Press, 1947.
    = 434.
    Also in 50, pp. 107–18.

368. "The Spirit of the Alphabet." *Catholic Art Quarterly*, 1947, pp. 80–85.
    Also in 47, pp. 346–53.

369. "Der barmherzige Samariter des Denkens" (über Ernst Michel). *Christ und Welt* 17 (25 September 1948): 12–13.
    = 373.

370. "Predigt eines Laien in Amerika." Zum Unabhängigkeitstag. Das Gesetz der Freiheit. *Christ und Welt*, 3 December 1948, p. 11.
    Also in 47, pp. 304–10.

371. "What Is the City Doing to Christian Life? An Analysis of the Future Relation between the City of Man and the City of God." *Religion in Life*, Spring 1948, pp. 171–81. A Christian quarterly of opinion and discussion.

See **374** (translation).

Also in **46**, pp. 221–34 ("Die Grossstadt"); **68** (no. 6, "Our Urban Goggles").

372. "Outside the Church." *The Parish Messenger*, Church of Saint James the Less, New York. December 1948.

373. Review of Ernst Michel's *Renovatio*. Zur Zwiesprache zwischen Kirche und Welt, Stuttgart, 1947. *German Books*, pp. 10–14. Chicago: University of Chicago Press, 1948.

    = **369**.

374. "Was bedeutet die Stadt für das christliche Leben?" Über die künftige Beziehung zwischen der Stadt des Menschen und der Stadt Gottes. *Zeitwende, Kultur, Theologie, Politik* Jg. 21 Heft 4 (October 1949): 241–51.

    Translation from **371**.

    Also in **46**, pp. 221–34, **68**, chap. 6.

375. "Liturgical Thinking." *Orate Fratres* 23, no. 12 (6 November 1949): 529–37; 24, no. 1 (January 1950): 63–69. A review devoted to the liturgic apostolate.

    Also in **34**, pp. 277–93; **46**, pp. 465–92; **68**, chap. 7.

376. "Das Geheimnis der Universität." *Die Sammlung*. Zeitschrift für Kultur und Erziehung Göttingen. Jg. 5 Heft 9 (1950): 523–39. Also appeared as a reprint.

    Also in **43**, pp. 17–37.

377. "Salamis und die Thermopylen." Ein Beitrag zur Erneuerung der Universität. *Deutsche Universitätszeitung* Jg. 5 Heft V/3 (1950): 4–5.

    = **176**, enlarged ("Akademik oder Argonautik").

378. "William James. Der Philosoph des amerikanischen Lebens." *Thema*. Zeitschrift für die Einheit der Kultur (Gauting bei München). February 1950, pp. 3–5.

    Also in **52**, pp. 20–34 ("The Soul of William James").

379. "Vivit Deus." *In Memoriam Ernst Lohmeyer*, pp. 250–60. Edited by Werner Schmauch. Stuttgart: Evangelisches Verlagswerk GmbH, 1951.

    Also in **43**, pp. 274–82.

380. "Die Weltzeituhr." *Hinterländer Geschichtsblätter*. Mitteilungen aus Geschichte und Heimatkunde d. Kreises Biedenkopf Vereinsblatt d. Geschichtsvereins für den Kreis Biedenkopf, 5.4.[1952?], Four Wells,

Norwich, Vt.

= **35**, pp. 525–27.

381. "Das Gesetz der Technik." *Darmstädter Gespräch, Mensch und Technik,* ɲp. 49–52, 173–79. Edited by Hans Schwippert. Darmstadt: Neue Darmstädter Verlagsanstalt, 1952.

See **427**.

382. "Der Gast." *Nutzen und Ordnung.* Gegenwartsfragen der Forschung, Lehre und Beratung für Wirtschaft, Haushalt und Familie. Jg. 4 Heft 8 (1953): 229–30.

383. "Reflektionen über das Thema Quatember." *Quatember.* Evangelische Jahresbriefe. Heft 2, Kassel (1953): 122–25.

Also in **43**, pp. 129–33.

384. "Jakob Grimm und unser Erlebnis der deutschen Sprache." *Der Evangelische Erzieher.* Zeitschrift für Pädagogik und Theologie. Jg. 5, Frankfurt a.M. (1953): 98–108.

Also in **43**, pp. 113–28 ("Jakob Grimms Sprachlosigkeit").

385. "Glückhafte Schuld." *Quatember* Heft 2 (1954): 94–96.

Also in **43**, pp. 146–48; **46**, pp. 251–55.

386. "The Homecoming of Society." *Adult Education,* pp. 76–83. Erwachsenenbildung UNESCO International Conference in Hamburg, 1952. Edited in 1954.

= **387** (in part).

387. "Die Heimkehr der Gesellschaft." *Adult Education,* pp. 76–81. Erwachsenenbildung UNESCO International Conference in Hamburg, 1952. Edited in 1954.

= **386** (in part).

388. "Pentecost and Mission." *Hartford Seminary Foundation Bulletin,* Winter 1954–55, pp. 17–25.

See **389**.

Also in **43**, pp. 236–43 ("Pfingsten und Mission").

389. "Drei Gaben des Heiligen Geistes." *Christ und Welt* Jg. 8 (May 1955).

Translation of **388**.

Also in **43**, pp. 236–43 ("Pfingsten und Mission").

390. "Raumzeit oder Zeitraum?" *Neue Deutsche Hefte* Jg. 1 (March 1955): 939–44.

Also in **43**, pp. 262–73.

391. "Glaube und Hoffnung. Ein Nachwort zu Evanston." *Neue Deutsche Hefte. Beiträge zur europäischen Gegenwart.* Jg. 2 (November 1955): 625–33). Correspondence with Gerhardt Bartning.
Also in **43**, pp. 262–73.

392. "Die Sprache des Westens." *Geschichte in Wissenschaft und Unterricht.* Zeitschrift des Verbandes der Geschichtslehrer Deutschlands. Jg. 6 (1955): 22–29.
Also in **43**, pp. 56–63.

393. "Das Christentum inkognito." *Evangelische Welt* Jg. 10 Nr 4 (1956): 84–85.
From **37**, pp. 185–89; paperback, pp. 152–155.

394. "Herakleitos von Ephesos schreibt an Parmenides von Elea." *Arzt im Irrsal der Zeit, Viktor von Weizsäcker. Eine Freundesgabe zum 70. Geburtstag am 21.4.1956.* Edited by Prof. Dr. Paul Vogel. Göttingen: Vandenhoeck & Ruprecht, 1956.
= Enlarged version of **52**, pp. 77–90 ("Heraclitus to Parmenides").

395. "Heraklit an Parmenides." *Evangelische Unterweisung.* Monatsblatt für kirchliche pädagogische Arbeitsgemeinschaften. Jg. 11 Heft 6 (June 1956): 94–95.
= **40**, pp. 26–30 ("Logos und Schule").

396. "Der Verrat im 20. Jahrhundert." *Die Gegenwart* Jg. 11 (3 November 1956): 697–700.
Also in **43**, pp. 64–69.

397. "Soziologie." Auszüge. *Wissen und Leben,* 7: 5–6. Stuttgart: Kohlhammer Verlag, 1956.

398. "Vorwort." Helmut von Moltke, *Die beiden Freunde,* pp. 5–13. Berlin: Karl H. Henssel Verlag, 1957.

399. "Tutilo of St. Gallen, and the Origin of Drama." *Catholic Art Quarterly* 20 (1956–57): 57–59.
Also in **47**, pp. 212–16 (translation).

400. "Sprache und Geschichte." Vortrag in der pädagogischen Akademie Dortmund am 20. Juli 1957. *Evangelische Unterweisung* Jg. 12 Heft 10 (October 1957): 153–59.
Also in **43**, pp. 86–93.

401. "Europa ist nicht mehr die nette Mitte der Welt." Wir denken immer noch in längst überholten Begriffen—Zum Beispiel, was ist schon:

der Staat? *Die Welt* 154 (6 July 1957).
= **178** ("Künftige Widersacher der Kirche").

402. Review of Henri Pirenne's "Mohammed and Charlemagne," trans. Bernard Miall (New York, n.d.). *The Muslim World* 47, no. 1 (January 1957): 74–75. Hartford Seminary Bulletin.

403. "Eine Generation allein ist nicht geschichtsfähig." Zum Generationsproblem (Zitate ausgewählt von Fritz Vilmar). *Ansätze.* Eine Semesterzeitschrift der Evangelischen Studentengemeinde in Deutschland, 11 November 1957. 3 pp.

404. "Theorien von gestern—Praktiken von wann?" *Junge Wirtschaft.* Zeitschrift für fortschrittliches Unternehmertum. 10 (1958): 426–28.

405. "Saint-Simon—der erste Soziologe." *Quatember* 3 (1958): 139–45.
From **39**, pp. 44–51.

406. "Ich bin ein unreiner Denker." Werbeheft. *Wissen und Leben* 11 (1958): 4–6.
Excerpts from **43**, pp. 97–112.

407. "Wer sind die Götter?" *Evangelische Unterweisung* Heft 1 und 2 (1959): 4–8, 25–29.
Also in **43**, pp. 283–94.

408. "Zeitbessernde Tage?" Eine Frage an die akademische Welt wegen "ihrer" Zeit. *Antaios.* Zeitschrift für eine freie Welt. Bd. 1 Nr. 3 (September 1959): 267–92.
Also in **46**, pp. 493–524 ("Was proklamieren unsere Kalender?"); **68**, chap. 8 ("Time Bettering Days").

409. "Furor Teutonicus oder Furor Classicus?" *Geschichte in Wissenschaft und Unterricht.* Zeitschrift des Verbandes der Geschichtslehrer Deutschlands. Jg. 10, 3 (1959): 133–37.
Also in **47**, together with **410** ("Das erste klassische Kostüm," pp. 357–67).

410. "Epilog zu: Furor Teutonicus oder Furor Classicus?" *Geschichte in Wissenschaft und Unterricht* Jg. 10, 7 (1959): 431–32.
Also in **47**, together with **409** ("Das erste klassische Kostüm," pp. 357–67).

411. "Tribalism." *Exodus*, Autumn 1959, pp. 9–24.
Also in **53**, pp. 121–36.

412. "Die Götter des Landes und der Götze Raum." *Werk und Zeit.*

Monatszeitung des deutschen Werkbundes. Jg. 8 Nr. 12 (December 1959): 7–10.

Also in **46**, pp. 172–93.

413. "Das Dreigestirn der Bildung 1920." *Die neue Richtung in der Weimarer Zeit*, pp. 61–87. Edited by Jürgen Henningsen. Dokumente und Texte von Robert von Erdberg, Wilhelm Flitner, Walter Hoffmann, Eugen Rosenstock-Huessy. Stuttgart: Ernst Klett Verlag, 1960.

= **91**. Also in **56**, pp. 20–42.

414. "Die Ausbildung des Volksbildners (1920 bis 1921)." Jürgen Henningsen, *Die Neue Richtung in der Weimarer Zeit*, pp. 88–102. Stuttgart: Ernst Klett Verlag, 1960.

= Abbreviated version of **93** and **56**, pp. 150–67.

415. "Revolution, Soziologie und Universität." *Werbeheft*, pp. 3–11. Stuttgart: W. Kohlhammer Verlag, 1960.

= **156, 157**.

416. "Universitäten oder Schulen?" *Nobis*. Mainzer Studentenzeitung. May 1961, pp. 10–11.

417. "Eine Friedenswoche." *Züricher Woche*. Schweizerische illustrierte Wochenzeitung für Politik, Kultur und Wirtschaft. Nr. 42 Jg. 13 (20 October 1961): 1.

418. "Stalins Einebnung und die Chronologie der Weltkriegsrevolution." *Züricher Woche*. Schweizerische illustrierte Wochenzeitung für Politik, Kultur und Wirtschaft. Nr. 48 Jg. 13 (1 December 1961): 1, 28.

419. "Vom Staatsbürger zum Flüchtlingsstaat." *Evangelische Unterweisung* Jg. 16 Heft 8 (August 1961): 121–22.

Also in **45**, pp. 530–32.

420. "Das Volk Gottes in Vergangenheit, Gegenwart, Zukunft." *Juden, Christen, Deutsche*, pp. 198–220. Edited by Hans Jürgen Schultz. Stuttgart: Kreuz-Verlag, Olten und Freiburg i.Br., Walter-Verlag, 1961.

= **435**.

421. "The Generations of the Faith." *Hartford Quarterly* 3 (1961): 95–111.

Also in **46**, pp. 276–300 ("Der Ton der zweiten Stimme. Erster Teil: Jean Calvin, Eine Festrede"); **68**, chap. 9.

422. Interview, Radio Bremen (Irmgard Bach, 1958). *Bremer Beiträge*, pp. 106–26. Auszug des Geistes. Bremen: Verlag B. C. Heye & Co., 1962.

Also in **50**, pp. 127–47; **52**, pp. 166–81.

423. "Der technische Fortschritt erweitert den Raum, verkürzt die Zeit, zerschlägt menschliche Gruppen." *Materialdienst* 4 (1962). Pressestelle Bad Boll. Protokolle der Tagung 2. bis 4. März 1962. Der Leitende Mitarbeiter der Firma Daimler-Benz in der Evangelischen Akademie Bad Boll (Walter Hähnle). 14 pp.

424. Über die Verlegung der Fürstenschulen nach Westdeutschland." *Alma Mater Joachimica* N.F. Heft 12 (August 1962): 150–51.

425. "Der Glaube der Ökonomen." Hersg. Süddeutscher Rundfunk, Hauptabteilung Erziehung und religiöses Wort, Ostersonntag 14. April 1963. 11 pp.

426. "Die Ökonomie des Glaubens." Hersg. Süddeutscher Rundfunk, Hauptabteilung Erziehung und religiöses Wort, Ostermontag 15. April 1963. 13 pp.

427. "Mensch und Technik." *Die Herausforderung, Darmstädter Gespräche*, pp. 110–12. Edited by Heinz Winfried Sabris. Munich: Paul List Verlag, 1963.

= **381** (first part).

428. "Mündig, unbefangen, unentbehrlich." *Deutsches Pfarrerblatt* Jg. 63 Nr. 23 (1963): 570–72.

Also in **46**, pp. 110–18.

429. "'Im Notfall'" oder die 'Zeitlichkeit des Geistes.'" Für Margarete Susman zum 80. Geburtstag. *Neue Sammlung.* Göttinger Blätter für Kultur und Erziehung. Jg. 3 Heft 6 (November–December 1963): 518–30. Reprint, Göttingen: Van Den Hoeck & Ruprecht, 1963.

430. "Revolutionen oder Revolutionäre?" *Alma Mater Joachimica.* Zeitschrift der Vereinigung Alter Joachimstaler. Neue Folge Heft 19 (25 May 1964): 270–75.

= **157**.

431. "Protestantismus und Seelenführung." *Deutsches Pfarrerblatt* Jg. 64 Nr. 17 (1964): 460–61.

= **326**, pp. 224–28, 248–53 (excerpts).

432. "Time and Historicity of Man." *Philosophical Interrogations*, pp. 31–33. Edited by Sydney and Beatrice Rome. New York: Holt, Rinehart and Winston, 1964.

433. "Das Ende der Dialektik Ketzer-Papst, oder: Das Jahrtausend des Samariters." *Die Wahrheit der Ketzer*, pp. 206–13. Edited by Hans

Jürgen Schultz. Stuttgart, 1968.
= **439** (abbreviated).
See **441**.

434. "Rückblick auf die *Kreatur.*" *Rechenschaft 1925–1965*, pp. 95–105. Ein Almanach. Heidelberg: Verlag Lambert Schneider, [1965].
= **367**.
Also in **50**, pp. 107–18.

435. "Das Volk Gottes in Gegenwart, Vergangenheit und Zukunft." *Freiburger Rundbrief.* Beiträge zur Förderung der Freundschaft zwischen dem Alten und dem Neuen Gottesvolk im Geiste beider Testamente. Jg. 16 Nr. 11, 61/64 (July 1965): 69–76.
= **420**.

436. "Die 'Objektiven Unwahrheiten des Bischofs Dr. Otto Dibelius.'" *Darmstädter Blätter* 9 (1966): 46.

437. "Buch und Funk." *Hundert Jahre Kohlhammer 1866–1966*, pp. 252–59. Stuttgart, Berlin, Cologne, Mainz: W. Kohlhammer Verlag, 1966.

438. "The Cruciform Character of History." Five Tippet lectures, Stockton, Calif., 1967. 68 pp. (p. 67 is missing). Published as pamphlet, Norwich, Vt.: Argo Books Archive, 1970.

439. "Das Jahrtausend des Samariters." *Orientierung.* Katholische Blätter für weltanschauliche Information Nr. 7 Jg. 32 (15 April 1968): 85–87.
Abbreviated version of **433**.
See **441**.

440. "Die Akademie der Arbeit 1920." (a) Grundsätze über eine Bildungsstätte für erwachsene Arbeiter (p. 85). (b) Die Stellung der Akademie unter den anderen Schulen (p. 90). *Zur Geschichte der Arbeiterbildung*, pp. 85–92. Edited by Dr. Hildegard Feidel-Merz. Bad Heilbronn/OBB: Verlag Julius Klinkhardt, 1968.
= **56**, pp. 92–98, 115–18; **339** (abbreviated); **340** (abbreviated).

441. "Heretic and Pope." Translated by James Burtness. *Christianity and Freedom* 7 (Spring 1968): 127–31. Augsburg College, Minneapolis, Minn.
See **433, 439**.

442. "Exil." Translation of *Hugo von St. Victor. 12. Jh. Vergangen-Erlebt-Überwunden, Schicksale der Familie Bonhöffer*, p. 119. Edited by Sabine Leibholz-Bonhöffer. Wuppertal-Barmen: Johannes Kiefel Verlag, 1968.

443. "Zukunftsglaube." *Deutsches Pfarrerblatt* Nr. 6 Jg. 70 (1970). 12 pp. Ein Brevier für Futurologen. Compiled by Dr. Georg Müller from Rosenstock-Huessy's writings.

444. "Zwei oder Drei in meinem Namen." *Christ in der Gegenwart.* Katholische Wochenschrift, Freiburg. 25 (19 July 1977): 205–6. Thoughts of Eugen Rosenstock-Huessy, selected by Franz Utt from *Der Atem des Geistes, Soziologie II,* and *Das Geheimnis der Universität.* = **174**.

445. "Eugen Rosenstock-Huessy über die Akzente seiner geschichtlichen Erfahrung" (from letters to Georg Müller). *Alma Mater Joachimica,* Zeitschrift der Vereinigung alter Joachimsthaler e.V. N.F. 37 (March 1974): 721–28.

See **456** (May 1973).

446. "Zeitgeist, Mythos, Krieg." 15 September 1956. Herausgabe der Eugen Rosenstock-Huessy-Gesellschaft, 1980. 16 pp.

447. "Militia Academica" (1933). Herausgabe der Eugen Rosenstock-Huessy-Gesellschaft, 1980. 13 pp.

448. "Ökonomen." Zum Thema: Der Glaube der Ökonomen und die Ökonomie des Glaubens. Vortrag in der Aula der Heidelberger Universität 1. July 1960. Herausgabe der Eugen Rosenstock-Huessy-Gesellschaft, 1980. 18 pp.

449. "Orientierung im dritten Jahrtausend." Heft 1, *Das Versiegen der Sprache.* October 1983. Edited by the E. R.-H. Gesellschaft, Peter Ohnesorg, and Jochen Lübbers. Apfelstrasse 209, 4800 Bielefeld 1. 37 + 2 pp.

= **34**, chap. 1, pp. 17–37.

450. "Orientierung des dritten Jahrtausends." Heft 2, *Namen und Gedanken,* pp. 39–62. April 1984. Edited by the E. R.-H. Gesellschaft, Peter Ohnesorg, and Jochen Lübbers. Apfelstrasse 209, 4800 Bielefeld 1.

= **34**, chap. 2, pp. 39–62.

451. "Orientierung des Dritten Jahrtausend." Heft 3, *Philologie oder Liturgik?* Edited by the E. R.-H. Gesellschaft, Peter Ohnesorg, and Jochen Lübbers. Introduction by Karl Johann Rese. Apfelstrasse 209, 4800 Bielefeld 1.

= **34**, chap. 3, pp. 63–82.

452. "Orientierung des Dritten Jahrtausend." Heft 4/5, Jenseits der Geschlechter, 1986. Edited by the Eugen Rosenstock-Huessy-Gesell-

schaft, Peter Ohnesorg, and Jochen LübbersG, Apfelstrasse 209, 4800 Bielefeld 1. 78 pp.

= 156; parts of **8, 42, 46, 415**.

453. "Hitler und Israel oder Vom Gebet." *Jenseits all unseres Wissens wohnt Gott*, pp. 147-59. Hans Ehrenberg und Rudolf Ehrenberg zur Erinnerung. Edited by Rudolf Hermeier. Moers: Brendow Verlas, 1987.

= revised translation by the author of **364**; **52**, pp. 178–94.

454. "Franz Rosenzweig und Eugen Rosenstock. Judentum und Christentum." Franz Rosenzweig, *Briefe*, pp. 637–720. Unter Mitwirkung von Ernst Simon, ausgewählt und herausgegeben von Edith Rosenzweig. Berlin: Schocken Verlag, 1935.

See **52**, pp. 77–170, with prologue and epilogue. (In the new edition, *Franz Rosenzweig: Briefe und Tagebücher*, edited by Raphael Rosenzweig and Edith Rosenzweig-Scheinmann [The Hague: Nijhoff, 1979], the letters are separated and inserted between letters to other correspondents.)

455. "Briefe." Martin Buber, *Briefwechsel aus sieben Jahrzehnten*, Bd. 2, Nr. (before **172**), pp. 213–15; Bd. 3 Nr. 242, pp. 298f. Heidelberg: Verlag Lambert Schneider.

456. "Briefauszüge." *Mitteilungen der Eugen Rosenstock-Huessy-Gesellschaft* Folge 11 (December 1969): 8; Folge 12 (June 1970): 16; Folge 15 (July 1971): 12; Folge 16 (February 1972): 11–12; Folge 18 (May 1973): 3–10 (on the stresses of his historical experience); Folge 19–20 (Spring 1974): 25, 27f.; Folge 21 (January 1975): 15; Folge 22 (November 1975): 4–13; Folge 23 (April 1976): 14; Folge 24 (October 1976): 4–11, 11–14; Folge 25 (April 1977): 6–16; Folge 26 (October 1977): 5–11. *Mitteilungsblatt der Eugen Rosenstock-Huessy-Gesellschaft*, pp. 20–23 ("Zum Naturrecht"), 1980.

457. Brief an Rudolf Ehrenberg, 26 March 1947. *Jenseits all unseres Wissens wohnt Gott*, pp. 105–6. Hans Ehrenber und Rudolf Ehrenberg zur Erinnerung. Edited by Rudolf Hermeier. Moers: Brendow Verlag, 1987.

INDEX